"I'm intensely grateful for th   al
and religious experiences t   ___, ~~~~natal
loss, my own professional fieiu. As discussions of these losses finally
become more commonplace, I worry that dads are being left behind.
This book tells loss dads, 'Your grief is important and you are not
alone!' I highly recommend *The Grief of Dads* to any bereaved man
looking for answers, for solidarity, or for ideas of where to look for God
in the shattering grief that comes with losing a child."

Abigail Jorgensen
Catholic bereavement doula
and professor of sociology and health care ethics at Saint Louis University

"It's more than OK for men to grieve. It can safely be said that if a man
does not grieve properly, there will be a flurry of other issues that will
arise in his life—physical, emotional, and spiritual challenges. The
men who have shared their testimonies of pain in this book will help
so many men who don't know where to start. I will be recommending
this book along with Ryan and Kelly Breaux's apostolate, Red Bird
Ministries, to those who are struggling with the loss of a child, whether
the child passed away in the womb or in their teens, twenties, thirties,
or forties."

Fr. John Paul Mary, MFVA
EWTN Global Catholic Network employee chaplain

"The powerful and moving testimonies of the men in this book who
have suffered the loss of a child, joined with similar examples from the
Bible and the lives of the saints, make this text a valuable resource for
men who share this experience. Would that I had such a resource in all
the years of my own pastoral ministry to help men navigate such grief. I
am grateful to the authors for helping us to understand the heavy cross
that they and men like them have been asked to carry."

Bishop Carl Kemme
Diocese of Wichita

"*The Grief of Dads* is a long overdue examination of the frequently overlooked experiences of men dealing with the death of their child. As someone who is intimately familiar with this type of loss, the resources and encouragement offered in this book give profound support to those men carrying this challenging cross. I highly recommend this book not only as a personal resource but as a valuable tool for small groups and parish-wide ministry."

Mary Lenaburg
Author of *Be Brave in the Scared*

"As parents who have lost children ourselves, we know this book is a beautiful, restorative resource. Dads—your grief is real. Allow the Lord to use this text as a way forward for deep healing in your life."

Jackie and Bobby Angel
Catholic authors and speakers

"Packed with rich stories and powerful testimonies, *The Grief of Dads* is a beautifully written book for Catholic men who grieve the death of a child. It gives you a roadmap to follow and permission to feel; a reason to heal and a purpose as you move forward, learning to live with your loss and your grieving."

Paul George
Author of *Holy Grit*

"*The Grief of Dads* opens hearts to the unthinkable reality of losing a precious child. Wisely grounded in our Catholic faith, it offers encouragement, enlightenment, and instruction—whether you are a grieving parent or a bystander who longs to reach out in compassion. It speaks the truth that we longtime bereft parents know firsthand."

M. Donna MacLeod
Author of the Seasons of Hope program

The GRIEF of DADS

Support and Hope for Catholic Fathers Navigating Child Loss

PATRICK O'HEARN and BRYAN FEGER with KELLY and RYAN BREAUX of Red Bird Ministries

AVE MARIA PRESS AVE Notre Dame, Indiana

Nihil Obstat: Msgr. Michael Heintz, PhD,
                    Censor Librorum

Imprimatur: Most Reverend Kevin C. Rhoades,
                    Bishop of Fort Wayne–South Bend
                    Given at: Fort Wayne, Indiana, on March 24, 2023

Founded in 1865, Ave Maria Press is a ministry of the United States Province of Holy Cross.

www.avemariapress.com

Paperback: ISBN-13 978-1-64680-253-1

E-book: ISBN-13 978-1-64680-254-8

Cover image © gettyimages.com.

Cover and text design by Christopher D. Tobin.

Printed and bound in the United States of America.

Library of Congress Cataloging-in-Publication Data is available.

This book is lovingly dedicated to St. Joseph,
to our departed children,
and to all fathers who have lost a child.

Amen, amen, I say to you,
you will weep and mourn, while the world rejoices;
you will grieve,
but your grief will become joy.
—John 16:20

Contents

Part III: Practical Wisdom, Reflections, Prayers, and Scripture Passages

Part IV: Tools for the Journey

Acknowledgments

We would like to thank our wives for helping us carry the cross of child loss: Thank you for sharing in the mystery of Christ's suffering in your own body. Your support made this book possible. We ask your forgiveness for the times that we have not grieved with you.

We would like to thank our children whom we lost and who prayed for us. This book is dedicated to you. Forgive us for the times when we have forgotten you.

We would like to thank our living children. You have kept us going.

We would like to thank all those dads who have contributed their remarkable stories of child loss in this book. Your stories made this book possible. May God reward you, and may you one day see his face and your child's face in heaven. In a special way, we would like to thank Jonathan Sumpter for his insights.

We would like to thank our editor, Eileen Ponder, for her fabulous edits and unfailing belief in this book, and Ave Maria Press for the opportunity to publish.

Finally, we would like to thank God, who inspired this book and who gave us the courage to write it. This book is for God's glory and honor! And we thank Our Lady, St. Joseph, and all the saints, who interceded for us.

Introduction

No one can prepare you for losing a child or the storm of grief that follows. It is like being in a small boat on the ocean on a beautiful, cloudless day when—seemingly out of nowhere—a vicious storm rolls in. The blue sky disappears and dark clouds overtake everything. The wind picks up and the waves toss your little boat—and you—up and down and sideways. You grab the oars and hold on for dear life as you row frantically. But you cannot see the shore. With each wave you wonder if this is the end—will you capsize and drown?

Grief is like the waves because it never really goes away. Sometimes grief is bigger and more threatening than at other times. And sometimes the storm of grief never seems to end, and you desperately search the horizon for a glimmer of the sun. In your desperation, you cry out to God like St. Peter during the storm at sea in the Gospel of Matthew: "Lord, save us! We are perishing!" (8:25). But even then, you are deprived of Our Lord's physical presence. You likely find yourself asking, "Does anyone know how I feel?" "Where are you, Lord?"

It probably seems as if you are alone because many around you have never gone through what you are now experiencing. Many appear not to notice your pain, or maybe they are afraid to address it with you. Even those closest to you, even your own pastors, can seem to think that you want to grieve alone or at least in private. They assume that time heals all wounds, but they are mistaken. No amount of time can heal you completely from losing a child.

When a child is conceived, the universe is forever changed, and when a child dies, the universe is likewise never the same. A part of your heart has been ripped out; the supreme fruit of your and your wife's marriage is lost. You may fake a smile, but inside the storm rages as the waves of anger, sadness, and sorrow continue to crash all around and keep you unsteady. While your wife thinks you are her rock, you feel as if your house is built on shifting sand. You grieve silently, you retreat in isolation, and the pain manifests itself physically. Your wife needs you more than ever, but sometimes you feel tempted to give up; your marriage vows are tested like never before. At times, you even feel abandoned by God. You are angry with him, the world, and those around you. As tears flow down your cheeks, you sincerely ask God from the depths of your heart: *Why did you take my child from me?*

Losing a child and the subsequent grief brings you to a fork in the road. Not just any fork, but one that involves one of the most decisive moments in your life. If you let it, grief will easily take you down the path of anxiety, destruction, despair, and bitterness toward God . . . even to the point of abandoning him and his Church. But if you allow God to enter into your grief, he will lead you down the road of empathy, healing, peace, surrender, and redemptive suffering. Like a rushing torrent, God's grace is waiting to break through the dam of your broken heart, which may have been closed for years now because of your pain.

Can a father really grieve with grace? And if so, what does that look like? Most men have been told, directly or indirectly, that shedding tears is a sign of weakness. From the moment we could walk, we learned that crying is for girls. We have been told to "suck it up" when we fall off our bikes, when we are hit by an 80-mph fastball, or when our first crush rejects us. We have been told to be strong for our wives and to keep our composure rather than show our emotions. We have frequently been told to accept God's will without questioning it and to recite rote prayers rather than to imitate Our Lord in the Garden of Gethsemane, who prayed desperately for the courage to align his human will with that of the Father. Yes, we have been told to "be a man." But what if the greatest joy in our lives is taken from us, sometimes instantaneously without even a moment to say goodbye? What if an ultrasound picture is the only memory we have of our child? What if our child died when they were three, ten, or even as an adult? Make no mistake, a father is never ready to bury his child.

Contrary to what our world too often tells us, tears are not a sign of weakness, but a sign of strength. If you doubt this statement, then read the Bible account of Our Lord weeping over the death of his dear friend Lazarus in the eleventh chapter of the Gospel of John. Jesus is the icon of what every man ought to be. We can also look to St. Padre Pio, whom the demons feared. His grief from losing his mother was so intense that he could not even attend her funeral, but instead locked himself in his room. Yes, the greatest saints grieved with God's grace. To not grieve for your child is to not be a true father. To not wrestle with God in prayer is to not be a true son of the Father. To never cry out to God in desperation and frustration is to not be authentic in your prayer life.

Each father's grief is unique—different from the grief of other men and also from his wife's. No one can tell you the right way to grieve. But reading stories from scripture, the saints, and today's fathers who are undergoing the same trials can show you that it is necessary, even healing, to grieve. Even though you feel alone and forgotten by many, God is with you in your boat, whispering in your ear, "I AM with you." And there are other men commanding their boats beside you, navigating the tempest with you in this, the most dark and bitter trial of your life. You may not see them, but they are there. And they want to help you steer your boat to the eternal shores of heaven, where your child awaits you and where Our Lord, Our Lady, the martyrs, saints, and angels long to wipe away your tears.

This book was written for all men who have lost a child, but especially for you. We want you to know that you are not alone, that it's not your fault. And although no one is grieving exactly like you, we hope the stories and insights from other dads, the spiritual and psychological tools for healing, and other resources this book offers will give you a sense of companionship with other men, and maybe even some healing and direction. We can allow the waves of grief to push us further away from God, or with his help, the wisdom of the Church, and the saints as companions and guides, we can allow the waves of grief to bring us instead ever closer to his heavenly shores.

Part I of this book is intended to help you better understand that you are not alone in grieving the death of a child. Many men today and through the long tradition of the Catholic Church have experienced much of what you are going through. We look first at what medical science tells us about grief, particularly about how men tend to experience grief. We then visit the stories of biblical and saintly fathers who experienced child loss and draw lessons from their lives and witness to the faith.

In part II, you will encounter the loss stories of ten Catholic men and how they each found their path toward healing in the traditions and practices of the Catholic Church. Part III provides practical advice for grieving fathers; for wives, brothers, and friends of grieving fathers; and for pastors and other priests. You will also find spiritual reflections, prayers, and scripture passages to help you in your grieving.

Part IV offers you a few tools for your journey toward healing, such as mood-screening inventories, space for journaling, and suggestions about where to find additional help. You can read *The Grief of Dads* from beginning to end, or you can select those stories, reflections, and tools that speak to your soul at any given time.

Part 1
YOU'RE NOT ALONE

1

Male Grief Examined

Child Loss Numbers

Losing a child is likely the most devastating experience of your life. The loss, typically sudden, left you heartbroken, angry, confused, numb, rejected. You may have suffered mentally and physically, and your marriage may have become stressed. The grief was real, but you didn't know how to express it; you felt isolated. You're not alone! Millions of men are grieving from child loss, whether it is from miscarriage, stillbirth, or the death of an infant, young child, teen, or adult child. Here are some numbers:

- Miscarriage, loss before 20 weeks gestation, occurs in about 1 in 4 pregnancies worldwide.[1]

- Stillbirth, loss after 20–24 weeks gestation, occurs in nearly 3 million pregnancies annually around the world. More than 1 million of those stillbirths (33 percent) occur during labor.[2]

- Among the 133 million babies born alive worldwide each year, 2.8 million die in the first week of life.[3]

- In the United States, in 2019, approximately 10,000 children died between the ages of 1 and 14, and another 10,000 died between the ages of 15 and 19.

- In the United States, roughly 3,000 adults between the ages of 25 and 34 die annually.

The number of men all over the world facing the grief of child loss on any given day is seemingly incalculable. As men, how do we deal with this grief? How does it affect us mentally and physically? How does it affect our marriages? How do we view our masculinity in response to our loss? How do we heal?

Grief Defined

First, what is grief? Most dictionaries define it along these lines: "deep sadness caused especially by someone's death" or "keen mental suffering or distress over affliction or loss." Grief and loss, especially human death, go hand in hand. In response to extreme loss, humans experience various, distinctive stages of grief. The stages noted below are often not sequential, nor do they have clear beginning and end points. But each stage does represent a general characteristic that most people experience when grieving. Understanding these general characteristics can help you understand your own experience of grief.

- *Denial*—the action of declaring something to be untrue. As you first learn of the loss, you may feel shocked or numb and question whether the news is true. Although your rational mind can see that the loss has in fact occurred, often your actions or behaviors take some time to catch up to that reality.

- *Anger*—a strong feeling of displeasure or hostility. As you understand the news to be true, you may experience anger, which you may direct at yourself, others, or God.

- *Bargaining*—an effort to negotiate the terms and conditions of a transaction. You may begin thinking about what you could have done to prevent your loss and consider making deals with God. Bargaining often comes into play with the news that a loved one is going to die but has not yet passed.

- *Depression*—feelings of severe sadness. As your loss concretely begins to affect your daily life, sadness may arise in varying degrees. You may experience crying, sleeplessness, or eating changes.

- *Acceptance*—the action of consenting to receive something offered. At some point you accept the reality of your loss, and although it still hurts, you're able to move forward in life.

After the loss of a child, a father is likely to cycle through these stages of grief in unpredictable patterns that are unique to his own journey of grief, but every man experiences a type of these characteristics in his own way and in his own time. The following is a review of the scientific literature regarding how men grieve and the effects of that grief.

Male Grief

Men grieve differently than women.[4] To us men, this is no surprise! But this difference is a major theme that appears over and over in the research literature. Many times men and women have been compared in research studies examining grief after child loss, with the resulting observation that the two sexes grieve in different ways, at different times, and with different severity.

Here are a few common differences:

- Men generally grieve less intensely and less enduringly.[5]

- Men typically cry less, talk less about the event, and generally do not find seeing a pregnant woman as painful as women do.[6]

- Men typically report less severe anxiety and depression immediately following the loss of a child.[7]

- Most men believe their primary role is to support their wives during times of grieving.[8]

- Most men feel more marginalized and less acknowledged than women following loss.[9]

Though male grief *appears* to be less intense than female grief, this is not always true and is very dependent on the unique loss of every man. For example, in a research study examining men's response to miscarriage, men reported higher levels of grief than women on a general grief scale—a result not anticipated by the researchers.[10] The result likely was surprising because social expectations encourage men to be stoic and unwavering. And this social expectation does reflect how men generally are less likely, compared with women, to accept support and outwardly display emotional reactions.[11] Of the men who grieve externally, many grieve alone with feelings of sadness, devastation, powerlessness, fear, and shock.[12]

Many studies focus on grief shortly after a loss, but men tend to grieve more after the wife has recovered from her initial grief.[13] In fact, from the time of loss until present, men are preoccupied by their loss in every aspect of their daily lives.[14] Men feel the loss of a child differently perhaps, but no less than women do.[15]

Not only do men grieve differently than women, but they also grieve differently from each other. Because men express different forms of grief, flexibility of support is necessary following a loss.[16] Grief is different for all of us because each of us has a different history. Our age, past trauma, previous child losses, length of marriage, issues with infertility, religious beliefs, living children, and many other factors can all impact how we grieve and how devastated or isolated we feel following a loss.[17]

Regardless of the circumstances, child loss is a significant life event for all.[18] The loss of a child changes the way we deal with grief and how we view the world. It also significantly affects how we respond to subsequent pregnancies, particularly with loss from miscarriage or stillbirth. Previous losses and struggles with infertility make the emotional toll even greater.[19] In subsequent pregnancies, negative psychological symptoms, especially anxiety, are profound, and yet most fathers want to be more involved in the obstetric care than they had previously been.[20]

After the loss of a child, men typically feel powerless. Particularly following miscarriage and stillbirth, the possibility of future pregnancies produces anxiety, and subsequent pregnancies produce constant fear of loss. Soon after the loss, there is internal and external pressure to delay or prioritize conception.[21] Following another conception, men understandably withhold telling anyone too early about a new pregnancy for fear of loss.[22] However, grief declines during subsequent pregnancies with routine confirmatory ultrasounds.[23]

Stillbirth presents the life-and-death paradox: the act of giving life through birth, and the death of the child during or before that birth.[24] Themes of grief common to men experiencing stillbirth include the centrality of hope, the importance of the personhood of the baby, protective care of the child, and the impact of the loss on personal relationships.[25] In stillbirth, many fathers regret not holding or spending time with their baby.[26] Stillbirth also leads men to avoid activities associated with the loss or other babies.[27]

Though most research on child loss is centered on miscarriage, stillbirth, and infant loss, in the few studies focused on adult child loss, the same realization resounds—men grieve. A major source of grief for all men is having to give up their hopes for and expectations of the child.[28] Maybe this theme helps explain the differences between male and female grief; men have something inherent in their fatherhood that only they can provide to their children.

The Physiological Effects of Grief

Losing a child affects us physically in a number of ways. By far in the research literature, post-traumatic stress disorder is the most observed effect and is pervasive across all types of men and child loss.[29] The trauma of child loss can lead men to engage in avoidance and coping behaviors, like alcohol consumption or drug use,[30] and the trauma can significantly impact eating, sleeping, self-care, and family-care patterns.[31] Research around child loss and post-traumatic stress disorder indicates that parents who lose a child have higher morbidity and mortality outcomes than adults who lose a spouse or parent.[32]

Post-traumatic stress can affect metabolism and lead to obesity, and it is well known for causing cardiovascular problems and sleep irregularity. Symptoms of post-traumatic stress disorder include numbness, memory decline, nightmares, insomnia, guilt, hopelessness, lack of focus, hallucinations, anger, self-destruction, shame, and flashbacks. A common symptom is anxiety, which can appear abruptly for short periods (panic attacks) or be present all the time (general anxiety). Anxiety may appear only during events connected to the child loss or may have no apparent connection to the loss. The physiological effects on the body that follow child loss are real and point to the need for physical and mental health support. (See part IV for mood-screening questionnaires and other resources.)

Male Grief and Marriage

How you grieve will affect your marriage. When Catholic men think about marriage, they think about children; the two naturally are united in each other. Prior to marriage, most men rarely think about child loss, and even if they do, they don't think it will happen to them. No father can prepare for such unexpected suffering and grief. After entering into this world of child loss, we authors realized that many men are grieving over their lost children, whether in the womb, at birth, or after birth. Meeting other men who are carrying the same cross of child loss helped us to better cope with our grief. Although we all experience grief somewhat differently, we gathered that most of us felt as if we were grieving silently.

Until recently, most research on child loss grief was focused on women, with a few studies examining couples. Recent research has more closely examined male grief, with two themes dominating: men believe their primary role is to support their wives, and men feel overlooked in the support process. We know that fathers are hurting and are, in fact, assuming a double burden in response to a loss. They experience their own pain of loss *and* the physical and emotional suffering of their wives.

Most married men want to be fathers. Men also want their wives to become mothers. Following loss, many men prioritize the grief of their wives,[33] and this often means that men delay grieving, even up to four months after loss.[34] Men feel obligated to disregard their own suffering to support the mental health of their wives.[35] In an effort not to burden their wives, to give them space, men also encounter loneliness; they don't know how best to grieve, or they struggle finding comfortable support outlets.[36]

Another prominent aspect of male grief is the feeling that their grief is only minimally acknowledged.[37] A lack of acknowledgment from family, friends, and health-care professionals means that wives eventually become the only support of grieving men, which can improve or harm the marital relationship. Some men reported the focused communication helped their marriage, while others reported more conflict and relationship strain.[38]

The fact that there are different grieving styles between spouses increases men's sense of isolation, adds to their grief, and leads to marital difficulties.[39] Plus, many times feelings of guilt become overwhelming.[40] Assuming you could have prevented the loss can fuel guilt, or thinking your wife could have done something can fuel spousal resentment. However, despite early conflict, learning to understand each other's grief can ultimately strengthen the relationship.[41]

Some couples report growing closer through dealing with child loss.[42] When parents are well supported, the grieving process can provide resilience, a more compassionate outlook on life, and a strengthened marriage.[43] Engaging in activities together, such as participating in a ritual for the lost child, can reduce the grief experienced by couples.[44]

Obvious from research and life experience is that we men tend to grieve differently than women, and women grieve differently than us, so we must be open to their experiences. And, importantly, "Fathers need support in their own right, rather than simply as an adjunct to their [wife]."[45]

Self-Concept in Grief

For many men, child loss cuts to the heart of fatherhood—having, protecting, and providing for his children. Questions arise, such as, What is it to be a man? What is fatherhood? Who am I, and what is my role now? With loss, some men feel as though they failed in their role as provider and protector. This perception, which often goes unrecognized, can have a negative impact on their self-esteem and identity.[46]

The stronger we desire paternal identity, the longer our grief symptoms last. And the longer we experience that paternal identity, the more intensely our grief systems persist. Our paternal identity quickens with the first heartbeat heard during the ultrasound, and this connection grows while we talk to our child in the womb, brush a young daughter's hair, or teach a son to drive.

With the questioned identity that accompanies loss, other questions arise. In particular, the question of "what if" consumes many fathers.[47] It's common to wonder what we would be doing if our child was here with us now. We may struggle when questions surrounding our identity arise in conversations with others. For example, do you include your lost child in the count of children when someone asks how many kids you have? Do you prefer not to?[48] As fathers, many of us want to speak naturally about our children, but to do so creates discomfort in us and others.

In addition to being fathers, we are husbands. Following loss, our self-concept moves to prioritizing our wife's grief—being more attuned to her sorrow, more compassionate, and more focused on strengthening the relationship as together we have experienced this tragedy. Grieving can lead to a new perspective on life and our own identity.

Healing

Support—we all need it, even when we think we may not. When we do want it, where do we find it? As mentioned earlier, a dominant theme for men is feeling that their grief is not acknowledged. Research shows that most men feel excluded from health-care services and follow-up support after their loss.[49] As a result, many men don't know that support groups exist for couples or exclusively for men experiencing child loss. Following miscarriage and stillbirth, men feel marginalized, particularly when people make comments implying that the child is "replaceable," as when they flippantly suggest having another or comment that it's better the loss occurred before birth.[50] Plus, many men feel that clinicians are not sensitive to the loss of a human being.[51]

Men who grieve externally tend to grieve alone or by developing distractions, like hobbies, which are often solitary activities.[52] Is this isolated grieving inherent to the way men naturally grieve, or does it stem from the fact that men are given less attention following loss? This question may be difficult to answer, but many men find it harder than most women to seek or accept help for mental health concerns, grief, and adjustment to loss.[53]

Upon deciding to seek or accept help, most of the time men rely on informal support from friends and family instead of professionals. This approach may be of limited help depending on their response. Finding friends who have experienced similar loss can be most supportive.[54] Some men have trouble talking to anyone about the loss, which partly may be due to a lack of community recognition and understanding. In these instances, promptings by another bereaved parent can open up a discussion of loss.[55] Of course, healing can come in many ways. Some men find healing by creating memorials of their children, while others focus on the future and ways to grow their family by various means, such as adoption.[56]

In general, men feel as though support resources are lacking,[57] which is why we decided to write this book—to provide a grieving guide for grieving men. In addition to the resources included in part IV, we hope that the stories and reflections included here help you find comfort, acceptance, encouragement, and peace, and that you come to know that you're not alone.

2

Child Loss in the Bible

Sacred scripture is filled with fascinating true stories from the creation of man to the coming of the Messiah, culminating in the redemption of humanity by Our Lord. Throughout the Bible, there are numerous accounts of normal people who responded heroically to the Lord's call and others who did not. One thing is for certain: to follow God, we must endure suffering, trials, and temptation—the result of original sin. In the words of Sirach, "My child, when you come to serve the Lord, prepare yourself for trials" (2:1).

Child loss is one of the most overlooked story lines in scripture. Having a child is seen as a great blessing from God. In the Old Testament, infertility was considered a disgrace; therefore, losing a child could be acknowledged as a father's greatest suffering. But somehow our world, those around us, and many in the Church have forgotten this truth. They mistakenly believe that a heroic man can handle any trial that comes his way, even if it means numbing his pain with fleeting pleasures. Many fail to realize that losing a child changes you forever; you are no longer the same person, for you now bear the marks of Christ crucified. Like Our Lord, your invisible wounds will never go away. No father wills to drink the bitter chalice of child loss: the child he prayed and longed for, held in his arms, tucked into bed, and taught to drive is gone. All that remains are the memories, some photos, and a small item or two that belonged to his child.

The entire Old Testament prepares us for the greatest child loss ever recorded—Jesus's death at Calvary. His death pierced the heart not only of his mother, Mary, but also of his earthly father, St. Joseph. Even though tradition tells us that Joseph died before Jesus, he knew the prophecies and thus experienced both grief and joy in anticipation of his son's future. Joseph likely knew what was to come and experienced grief because he would not be there to support Mary. His grief emerged because his beloved son and innocent lamb would be slaughtered, and he could not protect him. But Joseph also knew joy because his son was born to die for all humanity and redeem the world.

Every event and every person in scripture points to Jesus's Passion, Death, and Resurrection. And each of the canonized and uncanonized fathers presented in the Bible has participated in the Paschal Mystery. In a mysterious but very real way, each grieving father enters into the eternal Father's grief over the death of his beloved Son. In the movie *The Passion of the Christ*, God the Father's teardrop falls from heaven after his Son gives up his spirit. This teardrop symbolizes the Father's unfathomable grief, a grief experienced in a unique way by every earthly father who has lost a child. Only in heaven will we better understand the Father's anguish over his Son's Passion and Death on the Cross. For now, we must never forget that God the Father was overcome with sorrow at Jesus's death.

Adam

Although we remember Adam for his fall, God remembers him for his resiliency. How often we fall into error when we think, *I would never have eaten that apple.* Perhaps before some of us lost a child, we thought we were stronger than we truly are. Or when we read about some scandal, we think, *I would never have done that.* Instead, we ought to say, "Were it not for the grace of God, I could have done far worse. Lord, have mercy on me, a sinner." For those of us who have lost a child, we face a temptation similar to the one Adam faced: blaming our wives or others. We might think to ourselves, *If only my wife didn't have health issues, and so on, we might not have lost this child. If only the doctors did such and such, our child might have lived.* If we are honest with ourselves, we are no different than Adam. We can easily blame others for our suffering, even God.

Adam's fall and banishment from the Garden of Eden lie at the center of the book of Genesis, but overlooked is the story of a father who lost his child—or dare I say two children—in a horrific crime. Despite Adam and Eve's disobedience, God still blessed them by giving them two children, Cain and Abel. The murder of Abel by his jealous brother Cain certainly pierced Adam's heart. Abel died physically, while Cain died spiritually. Hence Adam would have mourned the loss of both children, though this is not explicitly mentioned in the Bible. We don't know exactly how Adam dealt with this blow, but there is probably no greater grief for a father than knowing his son was murdered by another son.

Scripture states that after the murder Cain departed from God's presence and lived in the land of Nod, east of Eden (see Genesis 4:16). We don't know whether Adam and Cain ever reconciled. If they did, it would have been a foreshadowing of the parable of the prodigal son found in St. Luke's gospel. The term "rainbow baby" designates a child who is born after a miscarriage, stillbirth, or infant loss. In a sense, Adam and Eve bore their own rainbow baby in Seth after the loss of their adult son Abel. Ironically, one of Seth's descendants is Noah, who was given the sign of the rainbow.

In the story of Genesis, we see how death, suffering, and original sin entered into humanity through the fall of Adam and Eve. Like Adam, we too must battle daily against the effects of original sin. Many of us fathers know the heartache that Adam experienced—to lose a child and see our dreams shattered for that child and for ourselves as well. In our sorrow, we must remember that our Eden does not reside in this world, but in heaven, the world without end. With God's grace, Adam was able to adapt to a new way of life for himself and his family, which involved toiling outside the garden. And those of us who have lost a child must also adapt to a new way of life, a life we would not wish upon anyone, but the cross chosen for us by God from all eternity.

Abraham

In the book of Genesis, we also read the story of Abraham. He and Sarah, his wife, were quite old when God blessed them with a son, whom they named Isaac. In a test of Abraham's faithfulness, God commanded Abraham to make of Isaac a burnt offering. Trusting the Lord, Abraham set out to do so. God, of course, intervened and Isaac was spared. The story of Abraham and Isaac reminds us fathers of how sacred our children's lives are and how the thought of losing them seems impossible. We cannot fathom the pain and fear Abraham endured, yet many fathers do experience the same sort of dread, knowing or suddenly facing the very real possibility that their child will die. A father whose son is sick and has been given only months to live, or a father who sees his daughter drowning and tries desperately to rescue her, knows something of the dread Abraham must have felt.

Every good father would prefer to die before his child dies, because seeing his child die is like dying twice. We all dream of growing old and having our children surround us on our deathbed. We long to say goodbye to them and thank each one of them while giving them our own last words from our little cross. But sometimes, this doesn't happen. Instead, we must vigilantly stand at our children's deathbed, handing them back to our eternal Father. The pain is so great because we cannot stop their suffering. We can only shield them with our prayers. And we would much rather take their place so that they might live longer. As seen in the story of Abraham and throughout the Bible, God's ways are not our ways, but he is always with us, even in the most dreadful of times. Like Abraham, we must trust that obedience and faithfulness will draw us ever closer to God, who knows how our journey ends.

King David

Sacred scripture tells us that King David had many sons (1 Chr 3:1–3). After his scandalous affair with Bathsheba, which resulted in her getting pregnant, David had her husband, Uriah, killed. But God was not to be mocked. The prophet Nathan told David: "The LORD has removed your sin. You shall not die, but since you have utterly spurned the LORD by this deed, the child born to you will surely die" (2 Sm 12:13–14).

In response, King David immediately began to fast and pray that God would spare his child. But the child, whose name remains unknown to us, died. Following his son's death, King David changed his clothes, anointed himself, and began to eat. One of his servants then questioned him, "'What is this you are doing? While the child was living, you fasted and wept and kept vigil; now that the child is dead, you rise and take food.' He replied: 'While the child was living, I fasted and wept, thinking, "Who knows? The Lord may grant me the child's life." But now he is dead. Why should I fast? Can I bring him back again? I shall go to him, but he will not return to me'" (2 Sm 12:21–23).

Like King David, many of us have tried to plead for our children's lives, but our prayers were not answered in the manner we hoped. God permits the death of David's son because of the king's past wrongful deeds. We might erroneously think that God took our child, especially in the case of a miscarriage, stillbirth, or infant loss, to punish us for some past sin like David. In truth, God wills the death of no one. But what if somehow God took our children to save them from something worse? What if God doesn't answer our prayer the way we like because he can see into the future and knows what is best? A father once complained to St. André Bessette that God was ignoring his prayers, even after praying a novena to St. Joseph. In response, St. André told this powerful parable:

> A man had three sons. That God might bless his family he came to the Oratory to make the novena preparatory to the feast of St. Joseph. Shortly after the novena his eldest son fell sick and died. The following year he decided to make another novena. His second son took sick and died. The discouraged father swore that henceforth he would never pray. One day as he was going on a journey, his car was suddenly stopped. An unknown man accosted him and begged him to come into the neighboring forest. There, the stranger showed him

> two corpses hanging from a tree and said: "Your two depart-
> ed sons, had they lived, would have become assassins and
> thieves and would have ended their lives on the gallows. Your
> third son is destined to become a bishop. See what grief and
> affliction would have been yours, had I allowed them to live."[1]

This is indeed a parable, and we shouldn't think that our children died because they might have ended up in hell. But grief must give way to mystery—ultimately to surrendering ourselves to divine providence. It was said by one saint that our lives are like flowers and God picks them when he chooses, when they have bloomed. Our time could be better spent praying than trying to understand why our child has died. Still, anger toward God is real and natural. As will be seen below, King David channeled his anger toward God with heartfelt cries. Acknowledging his utter pain and sense of being abandoned by God, David held nothing back from the Lord.

David appeared to move on from the death of his first child rather quickly, as Bathsheba, now his wife, bore another child soon after. They named this child Solomon. But David's grief would return once again and with greater force over the death of his son Absalom, even though Absalom had rebelled against him. Upon hearing about Absalom's death, "The king was shaken, and went up to the room over the city gate and wept. He said as he wept, 'My son Absalom! My son, my son Absalom! If only I had died instead of you, Absalom, my son, my son!'" (2 Sm 19:1). And further it was said, "The king is weeping and mourning for Absalom" (2 Sm 19:2). To be "shaken" implies a certain biological and emotional reaction to grief. This scripture passage evokes the grief of every father. At the same time, do not these words transport us to Calvary, where the Father might have said, "My son, my son!" as he saw his own beloved Son on the Cross? Unlike the Transfiguration, the Crucifixion does not bring forth the Father's voice; nevertheless, we might well accept that God the Father grieved for his Son there at the Cross, even as Adam, Abraham, and David grieved the deaths of their sons.

The greatest gift that King David gave the world and the Church outside of his descendant Jesus was the psalms. Psalm 23 is arguably the most iconic and remembered one with the words, "Even though I walk through the valley of the shadow of death, I will fear no evil, for you are with me" (23:4). Perhaps the Holy Spirit inspired King David to write this psalm while grieving the loss of his children. He lost several children, most notably Absalom and Amnon; the latter was murdered by Absalom for raping their sister Tamar. Anyone who loses a child feels as if they too are walking through a valley of shadows where death is all around them.

In another psalm we read, "Because of you friend and neighbor shun me; my only friend is darkness" (88:19). Or the words, "My God, my God, why have you abandoned me? Why so far from my call for help, from my cries of anguish?" (Ps 22:2). King David felt alone and abandoned by those closest to him—even God himself, in a foreshadowing of Christ on the Cross. When we lose a child or experience some trial, the psalms can speak to us in a personal way because we identify with the psalmist. We too have known what it is like to walk alone because some family members and friends have never experienced the sorrow of burying a child.

Through praying the psalms, we can learn to hope that God will see us through every trial. Psalm 126 says it best: "Those who go forth weeping, carrying sacks of seed, Will return with cries of joy, carrying their bundled sheaves"(6). God's grace eventually transformed King David's grief into joy and can do the same for each of us because we know that death is not the end, but only the beginning of eternal life.

Job

The book of Job is one of the most relatable stories in all of scripture because it addresses the question of suffering head-on. Little is known about Job, except that he was a husband and father. Some attribute the authorship of this book to Job himself, some to Moses, and others to one of the prophets. The book opens by describing Job as "a blameless and upright man . . . who feared God and avoided evil" (1:1). Job had seven sons and three daughters, and he owned thousands of sheep and camels and was very prosperous.

Job's children took turns giving feasts, where they would eat and drink abundantly. After each feast the devout Job rose up early and offered a holocaust for each of his ten children, for "it may be that my children have sinned" (1:5). One day the Lord had a conversation with Satan about Job, telling him that "there is no one on earth like him, blameless and upright" (1:8). Satan was determined to prove the Lord wrong. Specifically, Satan wagered with God that Job only loved him in prosperity but would easily turn his back on him in adversity. And so God allowed Satan to take away everything from Job, including his livestock and even his most precious treasures on earth, his ten children, when their house collapsed because of a violent wind.

Job's deep trust in God led him to say some of the most powerful words ever recorded, particularly from one who had lost nearly everything: "Naked I came forth from my mother's womb, and naked shall I go back there. The LORD gave and the LORD has taken away; blessed be the name of the LORD!" (1:21). No father who has just lost his children could utter such words without God's grace. Like Job's children, our children, in truth, belong to God and are ours for only a short while. If we work at being faithful and trust in God's ways even when we do not understand, we can learn to live aligned with this reality. We can learn to treasure the time we had with our children and keep them near in heart and mind and in our everyday living. Our sufferings can lead us to bless God, not curse him. Job did not bless God overnight. No, Job wrestled with God just as Jacob wrestled with the angel (see Genesis 32:25). He likely wrestled with God for years, pouring out his anger and grief, before he saw suffering's purpose.

It is said that Job never sinned, "nor did he charge God with wrong" (1:22). But others could see "how great was his suffering" (2:13). Later on, his grief becomes even more pronounced. Many saints have experienced Job's dark night of the soul. On top of his desolation, Job experienced the dark night of the body: "You have shriveled me up; it is a witness, my gauntness rises up to testify against me" (16:8). He had been stripped of everything and his body was racked with pain, reaching its breaking point when Job cursed the day of his birth. Note that Job did not curse God. Instead, the righteous Job looked into the depths of his own heart to see whether his sin had caused such punishment.

Afflicted with sorrow, and lamenting that his friends had abandoned him, Job wondered, "Have I no helper, and has my good sense deserted me?" (6:13). Was not Job's agony a precursor to the suffering of Jesus, who also felt abandoned by his friends in his time of greatest need? Many fathers can identify with this sorrow, this sense of feeling alone as the world around you and your friends move on, but you and your wife remain on the Cross. Job reminds each man who has lost a child, "Is not life on earth a drudgery, its days like those of a hireling?" (7:1). Fatherhood is a battle, and the loss of a child is one of the greatest defeats; it can easily end your marriage and lead you to abandon God if you are not rooted in him. But there is only one choice: turning to God. Job asks, "Who has withstood him and remained whole?" (9:4). Yes, Job realizes that there is no peace outside of God. To resist God is to resist true peace. Job further declares his faith and hope, now immortalized as a song: "As for me, I know that my vindicator lives, and that he will at last stand forth upon the dust . . . and from my flesh I will see God" (19:25–26).

In the midst of his suffering, Job seeks understanding, something every father who has lost a child ought to do. Specifically, Job wants to understand why God allows the wicked and wealthy to prosper in this world and avoid so much pain, especially child loss. After spelling out all the earthly blessings the wicked enjoy, Job reaches a clear conclusion: "They live out their days in prosperity, and tranquilly go down to Sheol" (21:13). Although contrary to the world's opinion, suffering is a sign of predestination for those who bear their crosses with joy, following their Master to Calvary.

Rather than offer comfort, Job's friends blamed his situation on his own crimes and sins. But Job knew that was not the answer. Instead, Job persisted in calling upon God, even though he felt abandoned by him at times: "I cry to you, but you do not answer me; I stand, but you take no notice" (30:20). When God does answer Job, he puts him in his place with these words, "Where were you when I founded the earth? Tell me, if you have understanding" (38:4). Any father who thinks he knows better than God the Father ought to recall this passage. Just because God's wisdom is beyond us does not mean we sit back and suffer blindly. No, Job constantly poured out his grieving heart to the only being who could understand—the only one who can heal a broken heart. Ultimately, Job resigned himself to God's providence. Even though death entered the world through sin, God wills the death of no one, for "dear in the eyes of the LORD is the death of his devoted" (Ps 116:15).

Eventually, God gave Job twice as much as he had lost in material goods. And Job was blessed to have seven more sons and three daughters. It was said that Job saw "his children, his grandchildren, and even his great-grandchildren. Then Job died, old and full of years" (42:16–17). In the end, Job had a blessed life, but not without sorrows and sufferings. Ironically, he and his wife had ten living children and ten deceased children. Though it is not mentioned, certainly Job would have grieved for the ten children he lost even after God blessed him with more children. Each child is unique; no child is replaceable.

Fathers of the Holy Innocents

"A voice was heard in Ramah, sobbing and loud lamentation; Rachel weeping for her children, and she would not be consoled, since they were no more" (Mt 2:18). St. Matthew uses this quote from the prophet Jeremiah to connect the ruthless killing of the children two years old and younger by King Herod to the brutal deaths of Israelites in the past. Today, the Catholic Church commemorates these children as martyrs on December 28, the Feast of the Holy Innocents.

Lost in this tragic story are the fathers of the Holy Innocents. We never hear anything about them—who they were and how they grieved. We see that Rachel prefigures the mothers of the Holy Innocents. But their fathers, along with St. Joseph, might well be thought of as special patrons of fathers who have lost a child. They are truly forgotten fathers; their grief is never mentioned in the Bible. Their wives' sorrow overshadows theirs.

The Holy Innocents shed blood for him who would later shed blood for their salvation, but perhaps their fathers blamed Jesus for their sons' deaths. Many thought the Messiah was supposed to protect them and even die for them based on the prophecies, not the other way around. They never imagined that their children would become innocent lambs taken to the slaughter. After all, if it weren't for Jesus's birth, their sons would have lived. We can identify with these fathers because we too, at times, may want to blame others for our child's death. In some situations our feelings may even be justified.

Ven. Louis of Granada wrote beautifully of the Holy Innocents dwelling among the choirs of angels, despite not having been baptized. He believed that Herod's malice was less powerful than God's goodness, so if that malice inflicted punishment where there was no guilt, God's goodness gave a reward where there was no merit. Yes, God's goodness always triumphs over evil. The fathers of the Holy Innocents may have been overlooked by scripture, but God never overlooked their pain. Their tears and our tears are not ignored. Just as God knows every hair on our head, so too does he know every tear that falls.

3

Loss Dads among the Saints

In the same way that every biblical event and person points to the Paschal Mystery, so too does every saint point to Jesus. The life of each saint is not a new Gospel, but rather, the beautiful unfolding of sacred scripture in time and space. The saint's mission does not end with death, but in a real way begins. The holy people in scripture and all the saints have an incredible mission to help us get to heaven by assisting us in our various struggles—sometimes the same battles they faced while on earth. Just because they crossed the finish line doesn't mean they've forgotten about their brothers and sisters who are still running the race. No, they cheer us on and plead to God on our behalf that we too might persevere as they did. They are the best of teammates and the closest of friends.

The saints seek us as much as we seek them. Just as we follow their lives, they follow our lives. In his great mercy, God has given us fathers particular saints to help us in our grief. God wants to introduce us to new saintly friends who desire to help us carry our crosses. Some of these saints are mentioned below.

St. Joseph

Feast Day: March 19

In the book *The Mystical City of God*, in which Our Lady is said to have revealed her life to Ven. Mary of Agreda, we get a glimpse of St. Joseph's grief during the trial of losing Jesus in the Temple for three days. Agreda declares:

> During all these three days he had suffered unspeakable
> sorrow and affliction, hastening from one place to another,
> sometimes without his heavenly spouse, sometimes with her.
> He was in serious danger of losing his life during this time,
> if the hand of the Lord had not strengthened him and if the
> most prudent Lady had not consoled him and forced him to
> take some food and rest. His sincere and exquisite love for
> the divine Child made him so anxious and solicitous to find
> him, that he would have allowed himself no time or care to
> take nourishment for the support of nature.[1]

Although St. Joseph lost Jesus for only three days, it felt more like an eternity. Many fathers have at some point entered into St. Joseph's grief, albeit for a few seconds or minutes, whether it is by losing sight of a child at the grocery store, in the neighborhood, or on the playground. Our minds often go to the worst-case scenario—that our child was kidnapped or even killed. But for those fathers who have lost a child, St. Joseph's worst nightmare becomes a reality that is lived daily.

The observation that St. Joseph almost lost his life from the grief of losing Jesus reveals that even the holiest saints were not immune to grief. Grief is *real*, and it shows no partiality to saints or sinners. Unhealthy grieving can lead to our own demise, mental and physical, especially when we neglect our basic needs. Like St. Joseph, many of us have faced a trial whereby grief decimates us physically. For some of us, the trial can end our marriage or lead us to reject our faith altogether.

Perhaps St. Joseph blamed himself for the loss of the Child Jesus on that trip to Jerusalem. Some of us might do the same. We say to ourselves: "If only I had been watching my child more closely, he would not have gotten lost. If only I had been there, my child might have lived. If only I did this or that, our child might still be alive."

In the fifth Joyful Mystery, we reflect on the finding of the Child Jesus in the Temple. Perhaps next time we pray this mystery, we can meditate on St. Joseph's grief, as well as Our Lady's (the third sorrow that pierced her heart). And let us in a special way invoke St. Joseph when we experience moments of "unspeakable sorrow and affliction" from the death of our children. But above all, let us never forget that our children, who became temples of the Holy Spirit at their baptism, are now no longer lost but have been found by our heavenly Father. God willing, we shall be reunited with them once again in the splendor of the New Jerusalem, in the Father's house, in the temple of heaven.

St. Augustine of Hippo

Feast Day: August 28

Although one of the greatest bishops and a Doctor of the Church, Augustine of Hippo experienced something few in the hierarchy will ever know—losing a son. Before his conversion, Augustine fathered a child out of wedlock named Adeodatus. The name means "gift of God." St. Ambrose of Milan baptized the boy at age fourteen, along with Augustine. Less than two years later, Adeodatus died. Augustine says nothing in his storied autobiography, *Confessions,* concerning his grief over his son's death. However, Augustine's grief at the death of his mother, St. Monica, gives us some insight into his pain. Monica died at age fifty-six, not long after Augustine and Adeodatus were baptized.

> I closed her eyes, and a mighty grief came flowing into my heart and overflowed into tears. Immediately thereafter, in obedience to an insistent command of my mind, my eyes drank up their source again until it was dry, and in this inward conflict my suffering was intense. As soon as she had breathed her last, the boy Adeodatus broke out into a loud lamentation, but after being hushed by all of us, he lapsed into silence.[2]

Certainly, Augustine would have grieved immensely over his son just as he did for his mother, especially since Monica was not there to comfort him or share his anguish. Augustine was deprived of the two people he loved the most: his mother and his son. When you lose someone, it can either make you long for God or despise him. Many people have been converted at the sight of their loved one's casket. They realize how fleeting life is. Although St. Augustine's conversion happened before the deaths of Adeodatus and Monica, their losses detached Augustine even more from earth and increased his desire to see God and his deceased family members.

Every father has a legacy to leave behind, not just for his living children, but also for his deceased children. The movie *Gladiator* comes to mind. The gladiator fights with all his might to honor the legacy of his slain wife and son. In a similar manner, every father ought to fight spiritually to honor the legacy of his departed child. Yes, a heroic father will do everything in his power and with God's grace to make it to heaven, not only to see the face of God, but also to see the face of his child. A noble father wants to make his son proud, just as a son wants to make his father proud. Our children spur us on to holiness because they deserve to have virtuous fathers. We can no longer live only for ourselves, but also for our wives and children. Before she died, St. Monica asked Augustine to remember her at the altar, and we can expect that the memory of his own son also stirred within Augustine's heart fervent prayers at every Holy Mass.

A father never forgets his lost child. He remembers them especially at Mass, where all of heaven joins in one worship. After losing his mother, St. Augustine felt there was "some immaturity in me that was leading me to the verge of tears." He felt that such "lamentations and groans" were not appropriate "because these for the most part express grief over the wretchedness of those that die, or even their apparently total extinction."[3]

Augustine raises a good point: grief must be tempered with grace and hope.

At the same time, a person who mourns a loved one's death is by no means immature, especially when it comes to faith. Grief and tears are not a sign of a lack of faith in the resurrection; instead, they are visible signs of how much we have loved and continue to love those who have died.

St. Isidore the Farmer

Feast Day: May 15

This eleventh-century husband and father lived a simple life on the outskirts of Madrid with his wife, Bl. María de la Cabeza (called "Maria of the Head" because her head is preserved in a reliquary, which is carried in processions when there are droughts). This holy couple was blessed with one child. The miraculous stories of St. Isidore the Farmer are well documented. As the patron of farmers, he would attend Holy Mass while angels plowed the fields for him. What is not as well known is that the couple's only son died during infancy. Isidore would have dreamed of the day he would work with his son on the farm, handing on both his skills and, more importantly, his faith. No details of the boy's death are recorded, but the loss of this child would have been a tremendous blow to Isidore and María.

Instead of giving up on God, Isidore devoted himself even further to prayer. If anything, the loss of his son intensified his faith, and his only task now was to lead his wife to heaven so that together they would see the face of God and be reunited with their beautiful boy.

In addition to engaging in a life of prayer, Isidore dealt with his grief by helping the poor, who dined frequently at his house. One time he and his wife ran out of food when Isidore invited more guests than they had the means to feed. Tradition tells us that God miraculously provided more food. Clearly, the vacancy in Isidore's heart left by his son's death did not weaken his capacity to love and care for others. In fact, perhaps it strengthened his resolve to do so. Sadly, the opposite is true for many men, at least at the onset of grief. The last thing we want to do is be around people, especially those who have never lost a child. Instead, we often prefer isolation, which the devil uses to distance us further from our wives and our community.

Because he lived so many centuries ago, many details of Isidore's life remain a mystery. We do not know how he grieved, but we do know that he ran to God instead of away from him. He ran to help his neighbor instead of isolating himself. Perhaps at some point he put all his energy into farming to forget the pain. But more likely, working on the farm helped Isidore to heal. It is said that Isidore's coworkers in the fields complained about him to their boss when Isidore was late for work due to attending daily Mass. But when the landowner saw that Isidore worked harder than the rest of the men, thanks in part to the help of the angels, he let Isidore continue going to Mass.

It must be noted that more than one angel helped Isidore plow his fields; perhaps it was his departed son's guardian angel together with his own guardian angel. Even though a child is lost, their presence never leaves. They intercede in ways that only God knows. Their pictures may be on the wall, but they are nearer to us than a memory, especially when we receive Holy Communion. St. Isidore was united with his son through the Holy Eucharist, which he received daily, and we can follow his example by meeting our children at Mass and most wonderfully in Holy Communion.

In some families, the gift of children is abundant, while in others it is scarce. At first glance, Isidore fell into the latter group, but he turned his grief into an abundant spiritual harvest, blessing all those who came onto his path. St. Isidore's tears of grief over the loss of his son watered the fertile soil for all he met, revealing to them that the greatest treasures are not found in this life, but in the world to come.

Bl. Henry of Treviso

Feast Day: June 10

Losing a child brings a pain no father should have to endure, but equally painful is losing one's wife. Some men never recover from such devastation, but this fourteenth-century Italian layman allowed God to turn his heartbreaking losses into something redemptive. Bl. Henry grew up very poor and worked as a laborer. Tradition holds that following the death of his wife and his young child, he "lost interest in a worldly life."[4] He could neither read nor write. When not working as a laborer, he devoted himself to daily Mass and prayer. He gave away all his belongings, especially to those more unfortunate than himself.

At the end of his life, Bl. Henry's only possession was a straw bed, from which many people took straw as a keepsake or relic following his death.

When faced with the loss of a child or spouse, we have two options: run to God or run away from him. In other words, we can choose to praise God or to blame him for the rest of our lives. It is often not a clear sprint to God, but a gradual returning to him day by day. In his later years, Bl. Henry became a beggar and kept only a little for himself. Redemptive suffering led Henry to imitate Our Lord by pouring himself out for others. Losing the two greatest gifts of his life when his wife and their only child died led him to turn his gaze toward heaven. Surprisingly, Henry did not join a monastery. Instead, the Holy Spirit guided him to use his grief to assist others in direct service. Yes, our scar tissue is not meant to be hidden from the world, nor should it be broadcast so that we seek everyone's consolation. Rather, our scars and losses are proof that we have loved and still love. They are proof that we are followers of Christ, for no one comes to heaven without suffering. Our scars are meant to help others heal by showing them that we have allowed ourselves to be healed by Jesus, the Wounded Healer.

St. Louis Martin

Feast Day: July 12

Many Catholic fathers dream of having at least one son. A son to carry on the family name or perhaps become a priest, a son to play catch with or go fishing with. Only a father can teach his son how to be a man, especially how to treat women with the utmost respect. Make no mistake, there is something truly special about a father-son relationship. But what if the only two sons you had died before the age of one?

That is the story of St. Louis Martin, the father of St. Thérèse of Lisieux. Not only did he lose two sons (both of whom he prayed would become priests someday), but he also lost two daughters. His fifth child and first son, named Marie-Joseph-Louis, lived only five months. His sixth child and second son, Marie-Joseph-Jean-Baptiste, who was born almost fifteen months after his older brother, lived only eight months. His daughter Marie-Helene died at the age of five, while his daughter Marie-Melanie-Thérèse (Melanie) lived less than two months. Their losses pierced Louis's heart and that of his wife, Zélie, with an unimaginable sorrow. Melanie's death was particularly heartbreaking because it could have been prevented. Zélie could not breastfeed at this time, so the family had hired a wet nurse. But tragically, the nurse neglected the infant and Melanie died. During these trials Louis had to be strong for his wife and his other children. Only God's grace could see him through losing four children in less than four years, something few fathers will experience in their lifetime. Oh, blessed crosses that turned this grieving father into a great saint!

Nearly a year after Melanie's death, Louis's nephew Paul Guerin was stillborn. Zélie wrote to her sister-in-law Celine concerning this tragedy, "You see, my dear sister, it's a very good thing to have little angels in heaven, but it's no less painful to lose them. These are the great sorrows of our life. How I wish I were near you to console you!"[5]

Those who have carried the cross of child loss are often more attentive to those who have been dealt the same blow, as we can see in Zélie Martin's words. The greatest sorrows, the heaviest crosses any parent will shoulder in this life, come from losing a child. And the sorrow never goes away. However, the cross becomes lighter when others reach out to help us carry it. Nothing is documented concerning how Louis Martin responded to his nephew's unexpected death. But we can well imagine that he offered support, especially prayers, because he wouldn't wish this most heavy cross on anyone.

A few years after young Paul's death, Louis buried his beloved wife, who died at age forty-five from breast cancer. Unhealthy grief can lead one to reject God and to premature death. After losing Zélie, Louis knew that his five living children needed him—especially his youngest, Thérèse, who was four years old at the time. Louis lived until the age of seventy. Clearly, death surrounded him, but he allowed his grief to become an opportunity to draw nearer to God, to help others who had lost a child or spouse, and to focus his entire efforts on getting himself and his daughters to heaven. Grief did not have the last word in Louis's life; grace and hope did. Louis knew that "the world is your barque, not your home"—words from a poem by Lamartine that Louis loved to recite to his daughters.[6]

Like every grieving Catholic father, St. Louis Martin likely experienced times when he wanted to give up as he wrestled with God in prayer and with harsh tears. The prayer of St. Teresa of Avila surely echoed in his heart, "If this is how you treat your friends, it is no wonder you have so few."[7] Louis was not a saint because he lived an impeccable life; rather, God, who is perfect, works through the imperfect, especially those who persevere through all the storms of life. God called Louis to be a saint and Louis responded. He could have abandoned the faith when his sorrows and sufferings seemed to drown him in an ocean of despair. But instead, St. Louis clung to the Cross, the only true anchor during the storms of this life, and called upon Our Lady, the Star of the Sea. St. Louis's great love for the Holy Eucharist and Our Lady guided him safely to the port of heaven amid the tempestuous waves of grief.

Servant of God Karol Wojtyla Sr.

In 2020, Karol Wojtyla Sr., and his wife Emilia's cause for beatification opened, only six years after their youngest child, St. John Paul II (Karol Wojtyla Jr.), was canonized. Karol Sr. had experienced the tragic deaths of his wife and two of his children over the course of twenty years. In 1916, his daughter Olga died sixteen hours after birth. In 1932, his beloved Emilia died from health complications in her late forties. Three years later, his oldest son, Dr. Edmund Wojtyla, died from scarlet fever at the age of twenty-six. Karol Sr. was described as saying, "Thy will be done,"[8] as he hovered over his son's casket. St. John Paul II once wrote about his father, "The violence of the blows which had struck him had opened up immense spiritual depths in him; his grief found its outlet in prayer."[9] Grief will find many outlets: addictions, anger, depression, despair, and even suicide. But prayer is the only outlet that brings true peace of mind and soul. Prayer as the greatest outlet of grief is seen in the life of Karol Wojtyla Sr., who often prayed throughout the night on his knees.

Losing a loved one, especially a child, the fruit of our wife's womb, will likely always remain a mystery. Why, Lord, did this happen? It is worth considering that perhaps, when God takes away someone or something, he wants to give us more of himself. Prayer is not likely to bring our children back from the dead, although a few miraculous cases have occurred. Nor does prayer take away all our pain. Rather, as with Karol Wojtyla Sr., prayer opens us up to God's healing grace and allows God to be God in our lives. There were certainly many nights when Karol Wojtyla Sr., wrestled with God in prayer, shedding tears of frustration, grief, and sorrow. After his wife's death, perhaps he wondered, *How, Lord, can I raise two sons without a mother?* And then when he lost Edmund, *Lord, what more do you want from me? Please spare my last surviving child, Karol Jr.* In the darkness, God is present, even though we don't feel or see him. Faith tells us he is there, dwelling in our souls. We are never alone, for the Blessed Trinity lives in us by grace first received in baptism. With God's help, Karol Wojtyla Sr., focused on raising a future saint rather than lamenting over the children he lost. His son needed him. We too are needed by our living loved ones.

Part 11

LOSS DADS TODAY

4

Miscarriage

Surrender Is the Only
Path to His Heart

Patrick O'Hearn

As I write, five and a half years have passed since my wife and I lost our second child, Thomas John, in June 2017 and nearly four and a half years since we lost our daughter, Angelica Rose, in August 2018. Both died in miscarriage.

Random texts from friends have come in frequently over the past few years, usually starting, "How are you doing?" I have not communicated with some of these friends in months or years, but I know intuitively what the text is about. Yes, they want to see how I've been, but really, they want to share the good news . . . their wife is pregnant. I don't blame them. There is no greater joy than finding out your wife is pregnant, just as there is no greater sorrow than losing a child. I only wish that more people truly cared or understood what it is like to have your child die. Perhaps this is because losing a child at any stage is not something most men experience, although it is also not uncommon. Those of us who have lost a child often feel alone, even isolated.

Prior to marriage, my wife and I talked about the many children we longed to have. We even made a list of more than ten names, including middle names. My wife came from a family of thirteen children, while I had only two older brothers. I always dreamed of having many siblings, but my mother was urged by her doctors not to have more children after she nearly died having me.

Following the birth of our first child, Jude, we were overwhelmed by God's goodness, and we couldn't wait to have more. We were convinced that giving our child a sibling would be one of the greatest gifts we could offer him, and when Jude was nineteen months old, my wife became pregnant again. We were so grateful and thrilled. Jude and his sibling would be twenty-eight months apart. We dreamed of him having a best friend to explore, build forts, and share a room with. We imagined that one day each might be the other's best man at their weddings.

So many dreams dissipated in one moment when my wife started to miscarry. We named our son Thomas John because we lost him on the feast of St. Thomas More. I knew miscarriage was fairly common, but I didn't think it would happen to us. We lost Thomas at around six weeks—we were shocked and devastated.

After losing Thomas, we told only a handful of people. Some would say, "I am sorry for your loss," while others expressed their concern and then immediately changed the subject, or only asked how my wife was doing. And others would say nothing. Because of the latter, I stopped telling people. Yes, I wanted some consolation, but the silence only augmented my grief. I thought to myself, *Does anyone care? Does anyone realize that we just lost a child?* To some stalwart pro-lifers, our Thomas seemed to be replaceable and too tiny to matter. They would say, "You're young, you can always have another one."

Months after Thomas's death, I recall driving home from work feeling frustrated with God, tears falling on the steering wheel. My once-joyful wife was depressed. The sibling we wanted to give Jude was no more. I wanted the good ol' days back: the blessed moments after Jude was born. I never saw my wife more joyful in her life, and the same went for me. God created her to be a mother and me to be a father. Make no mistake, children are the supreme fruit of marriage— the greatest gift after God himself in the Holy Eucharist. Looking into your newborn child's eyes is a tiny moment of seeing God.

When your child is taken from you, whether you held them or not, there is a void left in your heart. There is an indescribable pain that only those who have lost a child can understand. After losing Thomas, I cried occasionally, but I tried to be strong for my wife. Because she was struggling even more than me, I didn't want to deepen her pain by unloading my sorrow on her. So instead of showing my wounds, which would have brought some healing, I hid them from her sight. And as much as I tried to heal her, I realized over time that only Christ and a skilled Catholic psychologist could offer true healing. In fact, no one ever fully recovers from losing a child in this life. The mostly invisible scars will remain until we are reunited with our children in heaven, God willing.

I was unable to grieve in a healthy way because I tried to grieve by myself. I thought that being strong for my wife meant that I could not show her my emotions, especially my sorrow and tears. And therefore, I would only shed tears while driving alone. I was hurting inside and became angry with poor drivers for the first time in my life. On one occasion, I cried out to God, "Why, O Lord, did my child die?" Clearly, St. Paul's words fell on my deaf ears, "Therefore, I am content with weaknesses, insults, hardships, persecutions, and constraints, for the sake of Christ; for when I am weak, then I am strong" (2 Cor 12:10). Yes, we as men are most powerful when we own our weakness.

When my wife cried most nights, I wasn't always there to hold her. Selfishly I wanted to write, but I also didn't want to face the pain. I wanted some degree of normalcy. After a year of sorrow, I begged God to calm the storms from child loss. I wanted my joyful wife back. While we did grieve some together, we mostly grieved separately.

Going to Mass on Sundays and seeing large families, especially friends with babies, only intensified our pain. Seeing a pregnant woman had been such a wonderful sight before but was bittersweet now, reminding me of our loss. In the church parking lot, our little Honda Civic seemed so out of place with all the SUVs and minivans. These things had all become triggers of grief and reminders of what we had lost.

Thirteen months after losing Thomas, my wife conceived again. We had been praying so fervently to God for a rainbow baby (a child who comes after losing one). The news was welcome relief after more than a year of being caught in the greatest storm of our life. Having another baby after a miscarriage is the greatest remedy, though it can never replace an irreplaceable child.

Sadly, at around seven weeks, we lost Angelica Rose. We were numb. Did this really happen again? So much for God having mercy on us. What about all those couples who are not even married who are blessed with children? What about, God forbid, the one-night stands that frequently end up in abortion? God owes us nothing, but somehow, I still believed that if we lived a moral life, God would bless us with children. I felt like the righteous son in St. Luke's parable of the prodigal son.

After finding out there was no heartbeat at the ultrasound appointment, I went through some denial, one of the stages of grief. I thought if we invoked certain saints, our baby would somehow be saved. I remember pleading with our Eucharistic Lord and asking a few earthly and *countless* heavenly friends to do the same. I prayed for a miracle, as every father ought to, but there came a point when it was undeniable that this was another miscarriage, and our baby wasn't going to be saved. Even still, I continued to pray for at least a week longer. I had heard of miracles when St. John Henry Newman and Ven. Fulton Sheen intervened to save two unborn lives.

Witnessing my wife's two miscarriages and being helpless to save our children are the greatest sorrows of my life. When you are made one flesh in the Sacrament of Matrimony, you suffer with your spouse. Not only did our baby die, but our joy died as well.

Although I was upset with God, I never turned my back on him, which was only because of his grace. I also believe Our Lady kept me chained to her son by the Rosary. So many times, my prayers were uttered in darkness and dryness. But I had to keep persevering. I didn't try to bargain with God, though we did plan to make a pilgrimage to a Marian shrine in thanksgiving if we were blessed with a child whom we could hold. In fact, my wife and I, accompanied by our three-year-old son Jude, once drove seven hours to the Shrine of Our Lady of La Leche in St. Augustine, Florida, where many infertile couples have experienced the gift of pregnancy. We prayed a novena leading up to the trip, but there was no miracle.

What made the hurt even worse was having more friends announce their wife's pregnancy even though they didn't want any more children at the time. They were trying to avoid conceiving because they already had a few little ones and things were getting stressful. This increased my anger and at the same time my isolation. *Doesn't anyone see our pain?*

I slowly began to distance myself from friends who were having more babies, especially those who were indifferent to my pain. While having a child is the most joyful news, it is best not to share this news immediately with someone who just lost a child. But then again, would I respond differently if I were in their shoes? I hope so, but I can't be certain. We often do not understand people's sufferings until we have experienced the same cross. If we embrace our sufferings, then compassion and sympathy for others usually follows. If we do not, then anger and bitterness toward God and others usually follows. These insights allowed me to "forgive them, [for] they know not what they do" (Lk 23:34).

Another source of pain came from the lack of Catholic resources on child loss, specifically for healing after a miscarriage. I remember looking for articles online only to discover several Catholic writers adamantly express the viewpoint that children who die without being baptized are denied heaven and instead reside in limbo. One article even suggested hell for unbaptized babies, including those lost from miscarriage, according to some Doctors of the Church.

I wonder if any of those who advocate for limbo have actually experienced what it's like to bury their child. The theological debate concerning where my two children reside only intensified my grief, because sometimes I doubted that I would see them again. I wanted to believe that Thomas and Angelica were in heaven, but there was little reassurance in Catholic articles or from my pastors. Like the insensitive writers who champion limbo as a dogma, a pastor who fails to mention the pain of child loss from the pulpit only magnifies a couple's grief. Tragically, the silence from many in the Church gave my wife and me the impression that we did not lose an immortal soul, but only a body part, such as a tooth. Deep down inside, I also felt that many devout Catholics close to us communicated the following message by their words and silence: "Your children are in a happy place. You should be happy too. Get over it." I then asked myself, *Why do we prayerfully march to end abortion every January—merely to save these babies from limbo?* I don't think so. We march because we know that abortion destroys not only the baby, but also those involved. Child loss leaves an invisible scar on the heart of every parent, no matter the age or circumstances.

God did put a few priests and friends in our path to help us with our grief. These people entered into our pain. Through prayer, reception of the sacraments, spiritual direction, and reading the *Catechism of the Catholic Church*, I became more at peace that God knows where our departed children are, and I became more confident that Thomas and Angelica were with him in heaven. But they weren't just in any place; they were in the nursery of heaven, where our Blessed Mother lovingly embraces them.

This is also mentioned in the book *Heaven Is for Real*, the true story of a young boy who visits heaven and relates seeing Our Lady tend to all the babies there. But somehow there was a part of me that still doubted that I would ever see my children again. This was partly due to the silence of those around me, but also due to some ambiguity in the Church's teaching on the matter, particularly the theory of limbo. And yet, in 2004, Pope St. John Paul II asked the International

Theological Commission to study "The Hope of Salvation for Infants Who Die without Being Baptized." Joseph Cardinal Ratzinger headed the commission before he became Pope Benedict XVI. On January 19, 2007, Pope Benedict XVI approved the commission's findings, which beautifully concluded that there are

> theological and liturgical reasons to hope that infants who die without baptism may be saved and brought into eternal happiness, even if there is not an explicit teaching on this question found in Revelation. However, none of the considerations proposed in this text to motivate a new approach to the question may be used to negate the necessity of baptism, nor to delay the conferral of the sacrament. Rather, there are reasons to hope that God will save these infants precisely because it was not possible to do for them that what would have been most desirable—to baptize them in the faith of the Church and incorporate them visibly into the Body of Christ.[1]

Yes, the Catholic Church does in fact give hope to grieving fathers who have lost an unbaptized child. We must remember that God binds himself to the sacraments—he will act when the sacraments are properly celebrated—but God is God and not bound by them. God is therefore free to bestow his grace quite apart from the sacraments as well as through them.

Baptism is necessary for salvation, but it is not permissible to baptize a child who has died. The Feast of the Holy Innocents on December 28 gives hope to many grieving parents because we believe that these children are now united with Christ in heaven and gaze upon God in what we know as the *beatific vision* despite never having received the Sacrament of Baptism.

In my occasional agonizing over whether I will see our miscarried children again, my wife has reminded me, "God knows where to put them." Yes, our heavenly Father knows where our children are, but I pray that I can hold them someday. But for now, surrender is the safest and quickest pathway to healing. My children are not in some far-off place, but in the heart of my Lord. I had to learn that just because my grief became less intense and easier to handle doesn't mean I forgot about my children; instead, I was handing them over to the Sacred Heart of Jesus and his mother's Immaculate Heart.

One of the most beautiful quotes on this topic of child loss is attributed to St. Bernard of Clairvaux, a twelfth-century Cistercian monk and Doctor of the Church. He reportedly wrote the following to a couple who had experienced a miscarriage and, like me, had worried about their unbaptized child's salvation:

> Your faith spoke for this child. Baptism for this child was only delayed by time. Your faith suffices. The waters of your womb—were they not the waters of life for this child? Look at your tears. Are they not like the waters of baptism? Do not fear this. God's ability to love is greater than our fears. Surrender everything to God.[2]

Sometimes I want a different cross, or I want to come down from the Cross. There exists a real temptation to imagine what life would look like without this loss. At other times I have wondered what might have been if I married a different woman, without fertility issues, as have so many of my friends. The grass always seems greener on the other side. It's easy to love your wife when she's beautiful and fertile, but when she's bloody and broken, that's when your vows are really tested. St. Paul's words, "Husbands, love your wives, even as Christ loved the church and handed himself over for her" (Eph 5:25), struck me more than ever after losing our two children. Yes, I must lay down my life for my wife, but also join her on the Cross. She cannot grieve alone. She needs me and I need her.

Following Angelica's death, we went on a family trip to the Outer Banks with my parents and my wife's parents. I recall vividly how powerful the ocean waves were because of the hurricane from a few weeks earlier. At one point, a giant wave flipped me over and drove me head-first to the ocean floor, which could have caused serious injury. Grief has often been compared to a wave, but for the first time in my life, I could relate to this analogy. The grief doesn't hit you all at once. The waves of grief don't just come when you are in the midst of losing your child, but even years later. When I hear two specific songs on Pandora that remind me of Thomas and Angelica, I still get teary-eyed.

We switched parishes after a time because Mass had become a place where my wife and I were both triggered in our grief. Our former parish has a cemetery where Thomas is buried directly behind his sister. I recall driving home from a visit there one Sunday and just letting the tears flow as I saw all the large families buried there, but especially at the sight of my own children's graves. Not much has changed; we still have three children, two in heaven. Although the grief never goes away, we can see that grace has slowly started healing my wife and me. I recall one day breaking down in tears just seeing my son Jude play by himself. My wife and I want to give him a sibling more than anything. To see him play alone with his imaginary friends truly breaks my heart, especially since our son loves little kids. When he was younger, he would often bring a baby doll to bed, which was like a little sister to him since he really wants a sibling to play with. I often kneel before a statue of St. Thérèse on his dresser—since we believe with all our hearts that she answered a novena that led to his conception—and beg her to intercede for a sibling for Jude.

In my grief, I found a new spiritual director. He kept reminding me that God is in control. The sacraments, especially Reconciliation and Eucharist, were healing medicines the Divine Physician was using to transform my grief. With his grace, I began to slowly surrender to his providence.

When I noticed my wife was not improving, I suggested she meet with a Catholic counselor. After initially refusing, she finally gave in. Through eye movement desensitization and reprocessing (EMDR) treatment, my wife learned to better deal with triggers. One of the most difficult challenges for her, and at times for me, was having a good friend give birth at the exact same time our Thomas would have been born. Every time I see their child, I am reminded of my Thomas.

One day, my wife texted me and asked me to pick up some Kahlua after work. We started to return to some normalcy rather than being constantly swept to and fro by the waves of grief and suffering. We went for walks at parks. We began weekly date nights. We made trips to the beach, and we started to pray more spontaneous prayers together as a couple. We were starting to allow the Holy Spirit to bring joy back into our hearts.

Even though we have had two miscarriages, sometimes I think that my grief is not as worthy as that of someone who lost a child later in life. We never had a Funeral Mass for our babies, and there was no time to baptize them when they were alive. But then I realized that our deceased children deserve to be mourned as much as a child who was born. Loss is loss and pain is pain, no matter how many weeks or years we have known a child, because a person is a person, regardless of time. To not grieve for our children, especially those we have not seen, is to have bought into the culture of death.

In my suffering, I tried to listen to what wisdom I might find in our grieving. Besides understanding the pain of my brothers and sisters who also carry this cross of child loss, perhaps I can grow in humility knowing that God didn't give us the ten children we so longed to have. Perhaps I might have been puffed up with so many kids: "Look at me. I'm more pro-life than you." Perhaps devout Catholics look at my wife and me and think we are not pro-life enough. Some have innocently said to us: "How come you don't have another one? Is this all the children you have?" In our pain, I also realized something profound: only through suffering can you know your true friends and discover who you are. And just like Our Lord, who had fewer friends the closer he drew to Calvary, so too with us. Although many of our friends didn't know we lost children, partly because they were pregnant and we didn't want to tell them, they moved on from us. We felt abandoned by some family members and friends, who never asked how we were doing. While we did isolate ourselves from friends by not attending their baby showers because the pain was so tough, we also longed for them to see how we were doing.

Recent studies have found that women who miscarry suffer from post-traumatic stress disorder (PTSD). Without a doubt, I can confirm this truth as my wife was triggered by so many things, especially by seeing other pregnant women. Witnessing the blood of miscarriage, I found myself standing at the foot of the Cross with Our Lady as she watched her beloved boy, the fruit of her womb, Jesus, die before her very eyes. I may have never met my children and they only lived a few weeks in my wife's womb, but they were real. Sadly, I never got to see their faces, only their remains. Thankfully, we were blessed to have Angelica's ultrasound image, and my wife was able to hear her heart-beat—such a gift from God. To this day, I regret that I never heard my daughter's heartbeat or saw her image in person.

Can a father also experience PTSD from losing a child? Yes, he can, and I am proof. When my wife had her menstrual cycle after we lost our children, sometimes my mind would flash to the scene of her miscarrying Thomas or Angelica. When she cries, I am reminded of the time she called me from the doctor's office to tell me our baby girl had no heartbeat. Many fathers experience PTSD from a miscarriage, stillbirth, infant loss, or other types of death. No marriage preparation course can prepare you for losing a child. Most often we talk about the joys of marriage and do not address the sorrows. Grief is real. Grief is the Cross. And grief is grace.

But what made our miscarriages even more difficult to bear was a recent revelation. We discovered the presence of two toxic molds at our now-former house, undetectable in the air. Throwing away nearly all of our possessions was easier to stomach than knowing that my wife's mis-carriages likely stemmed from the mold. This only augmented our pain. I felt like Job, as the Lord had taken away everything that I held dear.

Reflecting on my own grief journey, I wish I had shed more tears in front of my wife. I wish I had just held her when she was in tears. I would give anything to have my two children in my arms rather than in God's arms. But I have slowly accepted that God's will is better than mine. At times, I still question it and wrestle with him in prayer, ask-ing why he allowed this all to happen. But I realize that surrender is the only path to his heart. I realize that the best friendships are when someone is authentic. This might sound crazy, but everything I have suffered in my life—I wouldn't trade it. Not because I love suffering, but because suffering has drawn me to my brothers and sisters who share the same cross of losing a child. Above all, suffering has led me to appreciate Jesus's wounds more deeply, leading me straight to his heart. As St. Bernard of Clairvaux says, "The secrets of his heart are revealed through the wounds of his body."[3] My grief and pain became Our Lord's invitation to his open heart.

Losing our two children gave me a glimpse into the eternal Father's grief over his Son dying on the Cross, a glimpse of Joseph and Mary's pain, and most of all, a glimpse into heaven. To this day, I still imagine what my children would look like. How I would have loved to teach my son tennis or twirl my daughter in the air. These memories I will never know. Our Lord said, "For where your treasure is, there also will your heart be" (Lk 12:34). Two of my treasures, Thomas and Angelica, await us in the nursery of heaven, and there my heart is.

This experience of loss and grief has made me realize that life is death. To live is to experience death. We are slowly dying to this world as God is detaching us more and more in order to prepare us for the world without end. At the end of my life, it won't matter what college I graduated from or how many children I had. What will matter is whether I loved and whether I learned to accept and carry the crosses God has allowed in my life with gratitude and not resentment.

For now, I must struggle with God's grace to persevere daily, so that maybe I can send a text to a friend months and years after they have lost a child and say, "How are you doing, brother? How can I help you? Praying for you on the anniversary of your child's death." They say misery loves company; so does grief. A husband and wife must grieve together. And they must never forget that God grieves with them even though he might seem absent, even when their family members and friends have left them. Let us recall the beautiful words from scripture chosen for the first reading at many Catholic Funeral Masses, "Dear in the eyes of the LORD is the death of his devoted" (Ps 116:15).

5

Miscarriage

Pray without Ceasing

Bryan Feger

We're pregnant! This was our first pregnancy; we were so excited! Marriage, kids, happy life—that's the plan, right? Until it's not. In 2014, at around eight weeks pregnant, my wife started bleeding; she passed our son while in the shower. I held him in my hand. He was less than an inch but already taking obvious human form. I was in awe of this little human being but in total disbelief of the situation. At the moment, I definitely didn't fully comprehend the magnitude of what was happening. Thinking about it now, I just want him here with me. We named him Cyprian.

No one ever plans on miscarriages or consciously accepts that having kids may be challenging, heartbreaking, traumatizing, or impossible. The incidence of miscarriage can be as high as 15–20 percent in the first trimester, usually resulting from genetic abnormalities, though knowing all the reasons is difficult since many miscarriages are not investigated. I knew this, and as a scientist, I thought I would stay objective about the situation. I thought, *Well, this is just the body's way of saying something was wrong.* No doubt, this was my way of coping—numbing myself and not attaching emotion to the loss.

My parents divorced when I was eight years old. At the time I cried, but crying gave way to anger in the following years. Then, without proper guidance to funnel that anger productively, I was scorned for being angry. My confusion about how to respond when hurt led to me numbing my grief. I say this because I think this happens to many men nowadays. Men in our culture lack male guidance on how to channel their emotions positively, especially anger; plus, our culture so often tells boys not to be sensitive. Therefore, numbing my pain or grief was my primary means of dealing with it. So I moved on—not positive, but hopeful that God would take our child into his arms because we had intended to baptize Cyprian. And I turned my hope to trying for another child, because in my mind there was no alternative.

After our miscarriage, my wife began having painful and irregular menstruation. While we were shopping for plants in a local garden nursery, she experienced the first of these painful episodes. She didn't feel good. Her abdomen started tightening, so we headed home. In the car, she was shaky and cold from the abdominal pain.

After reaching home, she took ibuprofen and lay down. I prayed a Rosary—scared and unsure of what was happening. Over the course of the next day, she vomited from the pain. The severe menstrual pain would recur with each cycle over the next few months. I felt useless. All I could do was be there, attend to and serve her, try to share in the pain. I prayed to Our Lady that she take this pain from my wife. Watching her go through that physical pain was excruciating.

We continued trying to conceive, but there was no sign of life. We used the Creighton model, luteinizing hormone strips, and temperature charts, and we saw a Natural Procreative (NaPro) Technology coach through our diocese. We used the best Church-approved methods we could find to inform our timing of the marital embrace, but no success. Two years passed. What could be the issue? By now fertility concerns consumed me. I spent many hours researching fertility methods and appropriate doctors. We decided to consult an obstetrical practice that specialized in natural fertility.

Based on my wife's symptoms, the doctor thought she might have endometriosis. "Might" because currently no confirmatory diagnosis can be made until a surgeon inspects the abdomen with a camera. Endometriosis is prevalent in 10–15 percent of reproductive-age women. It is a condition in which cells similar to the lining of the uterus, or endometrium, grow outside the uterus. The condition creates a hostile environment in the area of growth, thereby drastically reducing chances of conception, zygote implantation, and development. Removing the endometriosis, if present, would be our best option to improve our chances of conceiving.

During surgery, the doctors confirmed that my wife had severe endometriosis on her uterus, much worse than her symptoms indicated. The endometriosis was removed, and she was sent to recovery. The surgeons stated that our chances of conceiving would be best in the following months. These words brought a sense of urgency, although I felt confident that we would conceive shortly after my wife's recovery because of what happened while she was in the post-op room.

In the days before the surgery, I prayed a novena to St. Thérèse of Lisieux, the Little Flower. While in post-op, my wife's nurse began talking about gardening. We shared gardening stories for a while, and then suddenly the nurse became excited and said she had to share a picture of her garden with us. She left the post-op room to retrieve her phone and came back proudly displaying her photos. She said, "I had to show you my garden of little flowers. I have all these differently colored little roses." It didn't hit me until later how St. Thérèse had answered my prayers. My wife recovered beautifully, and we began trying to conceive again.

We're pregnant! The first full cycle after my wife's surgery we tried and, after much prayer, God provided. Although I didn't think the first miscarriage had affected me, I was a little nervous about the six-week ultrasound. Walking into the doctor's office, I was excited to see the ultrasound since we didn't see one the first time, but I also was thinking we might not see a heartbeat. However, statistically, what could be the chances of back-to-back miscarriages? The little baby's heart was beating well. I was so happy and relieved to see this little life. Sadly, two weeks later, my wife started bleeding. I tried to convince her, and myself, that maybe this was normal spotting. We went for an ultrasound; our baby's heart had stopped. Lying on the table, my wife wept; I stared blankly at the ultrasound screen. I was so confused. We named our second child Andrew.

How could this happen again, after two years of trying to conceive? I didn't know what to tell my wife, though I felt as if I needed to say something to relieve her pain. All I could do over the next couple of weeks was hold her and pray. I prayed to understand what God wanted from us, from me. Was this payback for my past sins, for going against his will so many times? We were trying to conceive according to Church teaching. Didn't we deserve children?

Questions like these swirled through my head daily, creating confusion on where I stood with God. On the other hand, these sufferings forced me to think more deeply about the reality of a supernatural God. I realized that suffering points to an intrinsic desire for a time and place void of pain, which can only be outside this natural world. Without God, my sufferings were meaningless.

I focused on consoling my wife and suppressing my emotions to give her all the room she needed to cry. I never truly grieved. I was sad, sure, but mainly for my wife, who suffered emotionally and physically—something I could never understand. I think my lack of grieving was frustrating to her; she may not have understood that I don't grieve the way she does. She felt as though something was wrong with her, that the miscarriage was her fault, that she was defective in her nature as a woman. All I could do was remind her daily how much I loved her and tell her how beautiful she was to me. She had gone through surgery and two miscarriages.

Through my wife's suffering, I learned that grieving is natural and that grieving as a couple is helpful for our relationship. I no longer numb or deny my grief; we grieve together. Enduring these miscarriages has strengthened our trust and our love for each other. Trust, because when you choose to suffer with your wife, she knows you will be there through any hardship.

About one year after the second miscarriage, my wife visited her nurse practitioner for a non-fertility-related issue, and the provider performed an ultrasound since she had not had one since the miscarriage. The ultrasound revealed a mass on the left ovary and a cyst on the right ovary. A repeat ultrasound two months later revealed that the left ovarian mass was eleven centimeters and the right one was enlarging, consistent with an endometrioma. Two endometriomas—one the size of a grapefruit. A month later, we visited a cancer obstetrician. Fortunately, cancer was ruled out, but this obstetric surgeon was the best at the robotic surgery needed to remove these masses. Following examination, the surgeon was very concerned, suggested immediate removal of the endometriomas, and scheduled surgery two days later.

I was terrified at the thought of my wife having to endure another surgery and recovery. This major surgery could very well end our chances of conceiving. As the surgeon stripped away the cyst, my wife's egg reserve would be harmed, and complete removal of her ovaries was not out of the question. Fortunately, both cysts were benign and removed successfully. After surgery, we again were informed that our best and possibly only chance of conceiving would be within the next couple of months.

We're pregnant! We couldn't believe it. God had allowed the previous suffering, I thought, so that we would better appreciate this new, beautiful life. We were six weeks in and anxious as could be. It had been nearly two years since losing Andrew. There was no reason not to be hopeful. Third time's a charm, right? We were going to a fertility clinic that would give us frequent ultrasounds to confirm the pregnancy. They knew our history and were sympathetic to our losses. Week eight came. This was it, the time of reckoning; if the baby was developing well now, then we were over a significant hurdle.

That day, my wife was certain the baby was dead and we would, yet again, not see a heartbeat. The trauma of miscarriage is real. When your hopes and dreams of raising a child are taken from you, every-thing about a baby becomes a trigger. Every ultrasound brings back visions of a beatless heart.

But this baby was alive! She was growing normally and on track for healthy development, so the fertility clinic released us and scheduled an appointment with an OB. This would be the first time a baby of ours had survived to the point of seeing a doctor outside the fertility clinic. This itself caused anxiety as we did not want to be released to a "normal" OB clinic.

At ten weeks, we headed to our new OB office. I was concerned about the baby, though my wife wasn't bleeding. She had begun pre-senting physical pregnancy changes in the previous couple of weeks, but in the days leading to this appointment, she felt as though the changes had stopped. Something was wrong. I had a bad feeling, maybe superstitiously, about this new office visit. The OB office said it wasn't policy to give an ultrasound at ten weeks; instead, they would just use the Doppler to listen for a heartbeat. They said sometimes the heartbeat isn't audible so not to be alarmed. We were hesitant because for weeks we had been seeing our baby on the ultrasound screen at the fertility clinic. We wanted to see our baby.

The Doppler went on—no heartbeat. Something was wrong. "Give us an ultrasound," I said. My wife started sobbing. The PA got the point. We got an ultrasound. The technician placed the wand. We saw our beautiful baby girl. Her heart was not beating. This was our third pregnancy and third miscarriage. My wife wept. All I could do was hold her; that's all I could ever do. Nothing I could say could console her; I knew that by now. I didn't even know what to say, not even to myself. My heart was broken.

About two weeks before our ultrasound, my brother and his wife told us they were pregnant. Their baby was about four weeks younger than ours. Having cousins close in age was going to be awesome! Plus, one of my best friends told us he and his wife were expecting; their baby would be about two weeks younger than ours. All of this news was wonderful! Everything was great, of course, until it wasn't. Knowing that our child would not grow up with these others was devastating.

This third baby was too big to pass naturally, so my wife would have to endure a D&C. We were back at the fertility clinic for this—crushed. My wife lay on the clinic table sobbing. All I could think was that I never wanted to see her in this pain again. I never wanted to try for another child. I was devastated and speechless.

With miscarriages, everyone questions why and wonders what happened. For the first time, we actually received an answer. We discovered that this beautiful baby had Turner's syndrome—a rare chromosomal abnormality only in girls. Our baby was a girl. We named her Hannah.

Hannah, in the Old Testament, was a wife of Elkanah. She had no children because "the LORD had closed her womb" (1 Sm 1:5). This tormented Hannah so much that she "would weep and refuse to eat" (v. 7). One day after dinner she vowed to the Lord, "O LORD of hosts, if you look with pity on the hardship of your servant, if you remember me and do not forget me, if you give your handmaid a male child, I will give him to the LORD all the days of his life" (v. 11). The Lord remembered Hannah, and she bore a male son.

Losing Hannah was different than losing Cyprian and Andrew. I felt sorrow like never before, especially as my sister-in-law's pregnancy developed. After my niece's birth, we flew down to meet her and celebrate her baptism. Holding her at three weeks old, I had the pleasure of rocking her and praying a Rosary for her life—just the two of us. As much as I loved this little girl, I couldn't help but think of what my Hannah would have looked like, how these two could have grown up together. Because I am an identical twin, there is a good chance my Hannah would have resembled her cousin. I felt a deep sorrow—sorrow for the loss of my child and the fact I may never physically be a father. At that moment, I thought of the sorrow our Blessed Mother had present before her all her life—the sorrow of her Son's death. I thought of my need to be present to my niece and be a father figure to her, so I continued to hold her and pray.

Who am I as a man? Where does fatherhood fit in? I had such a longing to bond with my children, hand on family traditions, help them grow into confident and caring adults. I wanted to have this adventure with my wife. I wanted to see her be a mother; I knew she would be so good, loving, and patient, and I knew she yearned to be a mother. My wife's pain and agony was probably the main reason I cried, but I cried. And it felt good. I finally cried, for all my children.

One of the times I was truly able to let go of my pain was during a Mass for infant loss and miscarriage at St. Anne's Catholic Church. While receiving our Eucharistic Lord, all I could think of was what he suffered for me. I felt as though I truly had entered, even remotely, into his suffering. Although sorrowful, I thanked the Lord for this suffering, for this cross he allowed. I praised him for this chance to prove my love for him. I desired to show him that I would endure suffering and not turn away from him so that I may be lacking in nothing. I held on to the hope that this world's misery would pass.

PTSD following child loss is real. And that suffering is lonely. I wanted to be heard. I wanted my pain to be validated. I wanted my children's lives to be recognized. Most individuals don't know how to react to miscarriage, partly, in my opinion, because even most well-meaning persons are numb to the human reality of an eight-, eighteen-, or tragically, sometimes even a thirty-eight-week-old child. The reaction, or lack of reaction, causes loneliness, even more so a few weeks after the news when barely a word is spoken so as not to provoke awkwardness. So you sit with the loss as a couple, alone. It's here that building relationships with couples or men with similar experiences of loss was so important to me. These shared experiences fostered a deep connection, an unspoken understanding of each other's pain, knowing that this person understands me, if and when I want to talk. Finding those friends was vital to my grieving.

In my office, I hung my children's ultrasound images next to pictures of their saint namesakes. The only shrine in America dedicated to unborn children is the Shrine of the Unborn at the Church of the Holy Innocents in New York City. On a visit to the shrine, I wrote my children's names in the book of prayers among all the other unborn children. I lit a candle and offered them up to Our Lady. These acts helped me feel connected to the reality of their lives.

Through all suffering, I always try to think of Our Lady, who personally knows what it is like to lose a child and so provides comfort to me. As St. Alphonsus de Liguori reminds me:

> So likewise had the Divine Mother to endure her perpetual agony that in all things, she, the Co-Redemptrix of the world, might be like to her Divine Son, the Redeemer. Mary revealed to St. Bridget that when she suckled her Child she thought of the vinegar and gall; when swathing him, she thought of the cords with which he was to be bound; when bearing him in her arms, of the Cross to which he would be nailed; when he was sleeping, of his Death. As often as she put on him his garments, she reflected how they would be torn from his bleeding body one day; and when she beheld his feet and hands, she thought of the nails that would one day pierce them, and then, as Mary said to St. Bridget, "my eyes filled with tears and my heart was tortured with grief." Thus truly had Mary to suffer and to be tempted like her Divine Son, so as to be able to succor them also that are tempted, and to merit the glorious title of the world's Perpetual Succor. Mary is now all-powerful in heaven, ever acting as our Advocate and interceding for us, says Blessed Amadeus, with her most powerful prayers, for she well sees our miseries and our dangers, and, as our most clement and sweet Lady, compassionates and succors us with a Mother's love.[4]

Praise be to Jesus Christ, now and forever!

6

Stillbirth

A Father's Grief Observed

Joshua Johnson

Fourteen years ago, I married a woman who is a twin from a twin family. At her family reunions, it is the singletons who are the freaks. So, sure enough, the first time we conceived, it was twins! We learned they were a boy and a girl. Surprisingly, the second and third pregnancies were singletons, another girl and another boy, respectively. So, when we found out we were pregnant a fourth time, we suspected twins. But God threw a hat trick at us. On that ultrasound there were not two, but three babies! We were shocked and admittedly overwhelmed at the thought of triplets. Then we found out they were three girls. Once again, we felt both filled with joy and also overwhelmed. The equilibrium of our family's gender balance—three males, three females (including us parents)—would be tipped forever by a surge of estrogen. But I have always been a pushover when it comes to little girls, and ultimately the thought of three precious baby girls brought us much joy. What a unique gift they would each have growing up together!

We were nervous about the high risk that comes with a triplet pregnancy—and my wife Katie was wondering how her body could carry three babies. But when we got past the twelve-week appointment, and then the sixteen-week, with all three hearts beating safely, we thought we were in the clear.

At the twenty-week appointment, everything changed. We were devastated to learn that one of the girls, whom we named Chiara, no longer had a heartbeat. The doctors told us that she would remain in the womb along with her living sisters and be delivered stillborn. Never having experienced the tragedy of a miscarriage, we were all hit pretty hard. One of my daughters made a paper sign that said, "I hate this day," and posted it on our front door. Very fitting, indeed.

As if Chiara's death was not enough, in the midst of this our doctors discovered that her sister Abigail had hypoplastic left heart syndrome (HLHS). We were not told much about it at first, only that through a series of surgeries she could have a relatively normal childhood. We learned we would have to temporarily relocate three-and-a-half hours from our home in Greenville, South Carolina, to Charleston for the birth and the subsequent surgeries. We were totally up for this, and we trusted that God would protect Abigail and were grateful that modern medicine could save her. We were so immersed in grieving Chiara that we did not do much research on Abigail's HLHS diagnosis.

This all changed two weeks later in a meeting with the doctors. We learned that there is no cure for HLHS, just temporary fixes, the final of which is a heart transplant normally in the late teens. For the first time we were told Abigail would be doing well to make it into her twenties. The prospect of Abigail's shortened life was like another death.

As the father/protector of my family, I found this news, though extremely difficult, much less debilitating than Chiara's death. While death might come sooner for Abigail than most, there was a lot I *could* do. And *doing* seems to hit that primordial instinct to protect and cultivate, to wield the sword and spade. Here was a chance to show Abigail and the world how much we loved her and how precious life is. We would roll up our sleeves and do what it took to save Abigail and help her live her shortened life to the fullest. Move to a different city where she can receive the surgeries she needs? Got it. Provide special care for her at home? We'll make it happen. Reorder our lives however we needed? Let's do it.

We had already lost Chiara, and that was the greatest pain we had ever experienced. We *could not* lose Abigail. I had a mission: to love. And this was not limited to Abigail, because I had a renewed fervor for life and fatherhood—for my wife and other children. Abigail changed our life long before she was even born.

But before all these new plans could be executed, we had to get her into this world safely. She had only one functioning ventricle, and to make matters worse she was a multiple who would most certainly be born premature. This meant she had little chance of surviving if born before thirty-four weeks because she would be too small for surgery. Katie needed to carry her to thirty-four or thirty-five weeks for her to have a good shot.

With the help of friends and family, we did everything we could to keep Katie in prime pregnant condition. Katie was a trooper in so many ways. She literally gave up her body for her babies, totally submitting herself to their needs. The rest of us did whatever we could. We received more moving help, donations, meals, and childcare than we could ever have imagined. From old friends in Greenville to people we had just met in Charleston, we were blessed to the point that we were never in need for a moment. We even had friends travel from as far as Washington State to help! After three weeks in the hospital to stop contractions, it seemed such a great victory for everyone when Katie made it to thirty-five weeks.

The birth of my three daughters was a peculiar mix of sorrow and joy. Sorrow for Chiara as we spent time with her body, joy for Bridget as we got to hold her, and a mix of sorrow and joy for Abigail, a name that means "father's joy." While we could not hold her as she lay in the bed of the Pediatric Cardiology Intensive Care Unit (PCICU), we could visit her.

The night before her first surgery, the meaning of her name truly came to fruition. Abigail was not only baptized but also confirmed along with her sister Bridget. After the downpour of grace, I held her.

Holding a baby is profoundly simple, but if there is one single hour I could relive in my entire life, that would be it. Scarcely can I ponder this moment without breaking down. For one evening, she was her "father's joy." In holding her, I did what every father is supposed to do: ponder the miracle of life we have been blessed with, enjoy that mysterious and sweet bond, and pledge to protect that child from sin and any other evils that might befall her. If our supreme earthly image of manliness is St. Joseph, let us consider that he does not hold a sword in his most glorious moment, but peacefully holds the Christ Child with his gaze forever fixed on him. That is fatherhood.

The next day Abigail's surgery was off to a good start. According to the first few reports, everything was going well. Then came the nightmare news no parent should ever have to hear. Abigail was dying. She had experienced cardiac arrest. Along with hundreds of others whom I alerted through our CaringBridge site, we began praying our hearts out that they would be able to restart her little heart.

When a team of doctors with somber faces entered the room, we sensed our hope melting away. The lead surgeon affirmed what we already dreaded: our six-day-old daughter, Abigail Rose, was dead. Words cannot describe the sheer pain of that moment and the minutes, hours, and days that followed. Our priest, Fr. Patrick Allen, came in after the doctors. He led us in prayer. After prayer, there were no words for several minutes. Just mourning. There was not anything he, or anyone else, could say or do. But his silent priestly presence provided more healing balm than words ever could. Fr. Allen then brought in each of our four children, from oldest to youngest, and shared the news with them. Now two of their sisters were dead.

Children are much more honest than adults about thoughts and emotions. They did not cry at first but questioned and denied that she had really died. This is indeed a common, almost textbook, first reaction. While our adult minds knew intellectually she had died, our hearts, our souls, our spirits could not yet absorb it. We could say, "Abigail died," but something inside had not yet accepted that. Children don't hide this; they simply express what is reality within their hearts,

that she did not die. That moment changed us, and we've been grieving the loss since and will for the remainder of our lives. Everything
is different now.

When we first walked into the hospital room where the nurses had
so lovingly prepared Abigail's body for us, words fail to express the
pain we experienced—and still experience every time we think about
it. As composure gave way to wailing, the only thing I could think or
say was "Our daughter, our beautiful daughter." Not "yours" or "mine,"
but "ours." The best way I can describe the feeling is that a piece of your
very being is torn out. As a father, this truly is what I experienced. My
progeny, my inheritance from God, the very life that we cocreated with
him . . . now has no life in her body. Yes, if we endure, we will see her
soul someday. Yes, that body will be reconstituted in the resurrection.
But we live our lives in the body, and feeling the cold body of your
child is such a violent departure from Eden that we can hardly take it.

Perhaps the hardest part of losing a child is that it is out of the
natural order. We expect parents and even some siblings or friends to
die before us. But our children are supposed to bury *us*. Not the other
way around. The loss of a child is also a loss of dreams. The rest of our
lives are filled with "lost firsts." Already, the firsts and milestones of
our beautiful baby Bridget have also served as bittersweet reminders
of Abigail and Chiara. We expect this will be true for every birthday,
every graduation, and every rite of passage we share with her.

Sadness is not our end; happiness is. Perhaps that is why there is
something in us that repels sadness from entering "normal" conversation. Talking to a grieving person is awkward, and it's especially
awkward with men. Silence is awkward. In *A Grief Observed*, C. S.
Lewis notes how people avoided him when he was grieving the death
of his wife and laments the stoic expectations of the England of his
time. Perhaps the more American way to deal with grief is to search
for a way to break the awkwardness. We often want to say something
that will make *us* feel better about the other person's grief. Americans,
as Alexis de Tocqueville noted, are impeccably optimistic. Optimism
has its place, but there are places optimism should not go.

Most of my friends gave me a great amount of love, sympathy, prayers, and thoughtful, wisely worded messages and greetings. However, with some men, I encountered a different attitude. They only asked how my wife was doing, without ever asking about me. While well-meaning, this approach implies that grieving the loss of a child is women's business. As if the stoicism commonly expected of men ought to go so far as to "bounce back" after the death of a child. One man even told me to "keep my chin up," as if there is no room for a man to grieve his baby.

Other responses were equally unhelpful. I know it is well meant, but please, don't compare the loss of your parent to the death of my child. I can only imagine your pain, but mine is different. I dread the day, but ultimately, I expect to bury my parents. I did not expect to bury my daughters. And I don't want to hear how time will heal. And no, God did not need more little saints in heaven. And no, dead babies are not angels; they are human beings whose souls and bodies are separated.

And no, while we have a well-founded hope that our unbaptized children are in heaven, we have no definitive doctrine. Don't get me wrong, I believe Chiara is in heaven. God's normative channel of grace is through the sacraments, but he does not limit himself to the sacraments. The God who created this earth out of nothing can wash away the guilt of original sin and bring a baby with no personal sin into heaven if he so wills. So it is with a great and reasonable hope that I believe that our Father in heaven will give this father the joy of spending eternity with Chiara. All this I deduce from what God has revealed about himself in divine revelation. But this is different from the situation of a baptized child, who divine revelation explicitly reveals is in heaven (she was baptized and never sinned).

I can tell you from experience that the death of our baptized child was different from that of our unbaptized child. It is not that we fear for Chiara's soul, but rather, that we did not get the blessing of witnessing the guilt of original sin being washed away, her soul being sealed, and her heavenly adoption. The lack of dogma on the fate of unbaptized children implores us to show our love for her by praying for her. We do this even as we ask for her prayers, trusting in God's mercy.

The fact is, we who have lost children don't want our children in heaven. We want them here with us. An early death was an affront to the Father's goodwill in creating them. Death separates the body from the soul and is an evil, one of the effects of sin entering the world. God did not intervene and stop the death of my babies, but he did not ordain it—theologically we call this his permissive will, as opposed to his positive will. We are grateful for our hope of heaven and the resurrection, but to self-canonize a dead baby discounts and glosses over a parent's pain. It may make you feel better to say a child is in heaven, but it is scarcely helpful to the parents. Was Mary allowed to grieve the death of Jesus? Faith does not ask us to deny the course of sorrow.

At the memorial and Funeral Masses, we chose as the reading the raising of Lazarus from John 11. When Jesus arrives on the scene, he becomes "perturbed and deeply troubled" (v. 33). But "deeply troubled" is a woefully inadequate translation. As both Fr. Patrick Allen and Fr. Jonathan Duncan explained in their respective homilies at our daughters' memorial Mass and funeral, a more literal translation is that Jesus bellowed like an ox. A mix of sorrow and anger.

In his divine nature, Our Lord foreknew he would raise Lazarus, first in this life and then at the Second Coming. So why does he express such strong emotion at his friend's death? Because he hates death. More than anything. Even knowing the glory and joy to come, he mourned and hated death like a man.

Jesus did not shy away from suffering, nor did he shy away from grief. In all this, he revealed his true virility—a virility that pours forth from a tenderness of heart, not from an ability to cope or "move on." Jesus's strength is found in his endless capacity to empathize, not in stoic endurance. Death separates us and causes a sharpness of interior pain like no other. As a perfect man, Jesus would have experienced the full truth of death and suffering, which means he grieved and hurt more intensely, not less. And therein lies his strength—he does not avoid the griever but immerses himself in the grief. That takes courage.

As a father, I want that same courage. Therefore, we who are grieving can take solace in Our Lord's example and make allowance for it. As I have led and continue to lead my children through this dark valley, I remind them of hope. But I have not hidden my sorrow.

The emotions, senses, intellect, and memory are a curious unity. Grief triggers, as I have come to know them, can come out of anywhere. I don't know much about PTSD, but I think the phenomenon is similar. You are busy going about your day, not counting on any time to grieve, and boom, something jumps at you and then the sadness and pain rush in. Sometimes it feels like a relief to indulge in the feelings of sadness and pain and let it out. Other times it is followed by deep depression. I'm not a psychologist, but I do know this—it is better to let these waves of grief have their way than to resist them.

Anger is also one of the cycles of grief. First, I became angry that the doctors didn't choose an alternative procedure on Abigail that could have kept her alive after the surgery and given her a chance at open-heart surgery a few weeks later. Because of Abigail, they are changing their approach with babies who have hearts like hers. (If it has better results, the head pediatric surgeon has told me he will call it the "Abigail method.") But the hell with that. Why did my daughter have to be the victim that changed your strategy? Of course, I know that I should be happy for any lives that may be saved in the future, but for now I am angry. Because of one stupid stent that could have waited, I lost my daughter.

But in the waves of grief that come, it is not the doctors I am mad at. In fact, if I were in their shoes, I would have made the same decision. If they had done the procedure dozens of times with no fatalities, and not doing the full procedure could likely lead to other complications, why would they have proceeded in any other way? Add to that they tried everything they could, including forty-five minutes of chest compressions to manually keep her heart going. I could see the pain in the doctor's eyes when we had our follow-up meeting. It was not his daughter, but she died on his watch—not exactly an easy day at the office.

Doctors have been given tremendous gifts to save lives, but life and death are ultimately not in their hands. God is a lot more powerful than any doctor. With the faintest effort, God could have not only saved Abigail on the operating table that day but also miraculously healed her heart defect altogether.

But he did not. In her greatest hour of need, in our greatest hour of pleading, he let death happen. He may not have caused it, but he allowed it. Despite hundreds of people petitioning for her, he let it happen. Doctors have limits, but God does not.

Intellectually and even in my heart, I know and believe that God can bring good out of evil and that I will one day praise him for his loving plan in allowing us to lose Abigail and Chiara. But I am their father, and the God of miracles that we prayed to so fervently did not save the lives of my daughters. How can I as a father not be angry at God?

So what to do? Should I shake my fist at God? Should I try to get back at him? Some people do this by abandoning their religion. I simply can't. At one point in dealing with his grief, C. S. Lewis jokingly wonders if trying to "stick it to God" will get him anywhere. He later remarks that it may cause him to lose the gift of heaven, and then he will never again see his beloved. While tongue-in-cheek, there is some truth here. Abandoning God will not do anything but hurt us. There is nowhere else to go but to God.

Even though I am angry with God that he didn't save Abigail, I cannot be angry with him on the whole. He did not need me, but he created me. He gave me life. He has forgiven my sins and given me a heavenly inheritance. And all this even though I have repeatedly let him down and offended him. He has blessed me beyond measure with a beautiful wife, four amazing children, and now a beautiful baby, Bridget. Not to mention good health and material blessings.

And yes, God blessed us with Chiara and Abigail. The day Abigail died, my pastor back in Greenville, Fr. Jay Scott Newman, texted me. As expected, he assured us of his prayers and that he was there to talk when we were ready. Yet one line jolted me: "God be praised for her life." Yes, there is a part of me that is angry God did not prolong Abigail's life. But as Fr. Newman later said in a homily, in the scope of eternity, eight months in the womb and six days on earth plus eternity is not less than eighty years on earth plus eternity. God did not need Chiara and Abigail. He created them out of love. Now they live forever. This pain, while real, is but a breath when compared with eternity. So yes, "God be praised for her life." If it means I have a life tinged with grief till the day I die, so be it. It is worth it for the eternal life she enjoys and, if I stay close to Christ, I will also enjoy.

A hundred years ago, mothers and children were more likely to die during childbirth compared to today. The same for childhood death, workplace death, death in war, death from diseases, and so on. Alongside death, there were a great deal more hard knocks in life. A hailstorm might destroy your crops. It may be a hungry winter. Can't pay back a loan? Debtor's prison. Injure yourself on the farm or on the job? Unless you have neighbors or family who will step in, your family may become beggars.

Today in our abundance, we as men can be soft physically but also weak when it comes to empathy, because empathy is learned in a culture that knows how to suffer well. It is not as if we made a conscious choice to be blind to the suffering and pain in the world. Instead, it is the outcome of a world where the death of children and spouses, starvation, hunger, and disease have been so greatly reduced that you are the exception rather than the rule if you experience them. Many of us are "out of practice."

So here comes one positive outcome of grief—it cuts your heart and reveals love. A love that you may have known was there but did not know was that strong. You did not know it was that strong because you had never been cut that deep. Once cut, the love flows more readily. This is what redemption has revealed. As St. Paul says: "Now I rejoice in my sufferings for your sake, and in my flesh I am filling up what is lacking in the afflictions of Christ on behalf of his body, which is the church" (Col 1:24). What is lacking is not Jesus's suffering, for that was accomplished "once for all" (Heb 10:10). As Christ's body, it is our afflictions that must come to fruition. If we are properly conformed to Christ, they make us more like him, which is indeed the entire goal of the Christian life. While not pleasant, cuts and wounds reveal love. This is the point of the crucifix in your church.

At the Funeral Mass for Abigail and Chiara, an insight came to me in the midst of great sorrow. I had received Holy Communion and was back in my pew praying the Anima Christi prayer, as is my custom after receiving Our Lord in the Eucharist. A prayer like this can become pretty routine, but this time, instead of trying to affix my attention on the crucifix, I was looking straight at golden urns housing my precious daughters' earthly remains in the sanctuary. In that moment the words "Within thy wounds hide me" hit me so hard that I could not get along in the prayer any further. I always thought of Jesus's wounds in terms of how they atoned and healed my sins, and to be sure, this is true. But in this moment, I realized that I was being hidden in the wounds of Christ not only for remission of sins, but also for a sharing in his own sorrow, pain, and Passion. Until Chiara's and Abigail's deaths, the degree of sharing in Christ's sorrow had been relatively surface level for me. But now, here, immersed in sorrow, I felt I was literally hidden within the wounds of Christ. His own sorrow, pain, and Passion now included sorrow, pain, and Passion for our loss. In his wounds we can bear all our sorrow. Jesus's wounds are the result of death—but paradoxically they have defeated death. The very thing he hates he endured himself in the most horrific kind of way. Could God have accomplished redemption in any way he chose? This is an interesting theological speculation, but the fact remains, he chose to do it by tasting the very consequence of sin itself: death.

And let us not forget Our Lady. The sting of death is a double-edged sword, one for those who experience it and the other for those who must watch them experience it. This is amplified when it is your own child who dies. And is there a more horrendous experience than not only watching your child die, but seeing his body beaten, torn, and left to hang before your eyes? God the Father experienced this as a true Father in all his divinity. Mary experienced this as a mother in her humanity but with the divine gift of faith. Yes, she was sorrowful beyond words. Yet in her sorrow she persisted in trusting God. Her act of faith in the Annunciation continued right through Jesus's Passion. We ask that we might follow her in trusting her son, even through the dark valley.

Our God is not one who is distant in tragedy, but one who draws closer, for he has gone before us in death so that while we too must die, we will one day put on immortality as he did. Yet those wounds will still be there—but his wounds, as hymn writer Charles Wesley puts it in "Lo He Comes," are now "glorious scars." Someday these wounds from losing our children will also be made into glorious scars.

In the meantime, I am hidden in his wounds in a way I never have been. This is why as I start to return to my duties I will not seek to "move on," but "move in." Move in, that is, to Jesus's wounds. Every time I see a picture, hear a song, or have a memory that triggers grief, I am not going to run away. I will resolve to run into his wounds. I cannot say that I will always do this as I should, but I am resolved to follow Christ in this way.

St. Paul tells us, "If one part suffers, all the parts suffer with it" (1 Cor 12:26). Seeing other men share in your grief is a strange but comforting experience. Our pastor during our time in Charleston, Fr. Allen, was with us at each moment of tragedy. As the time drew near to release Chiara, he came to bless her body. Before beginning the last rites, he spent time gazing lovingly and with sorrow at the face God gave her. Herein he witnessed to her dignity and shared in our grief. By praying the liturgy of the Church in this rite, he served as an instrument of Christ. Christ blessed us, shared in our sorrow, and gave us hope through him. Just three days later he was with us during those first minutes after learning of Abigail's death, sharing in our tears. Scarcely forty-eight hours after baptizing and confirming her, he returned to bless Abigail's lifeless body, just as he had with Chiara. I can still see the sorrow in his eyes.

What a calling our priests have—to stand in the person of Christ, not only at the altar, but at the grave. Fr. Allen's talk was no canned funeral homily about bad things happening to good people, but a lovingly composed message to witness to the truths of our faith. The same is true of Fr. Duncan's homily and his care for us during the Funeral Mass and internment in Greenville. We also experienced great kindness and pastoral care from our pastor in Greenville, Fr. Newman.

Five days after the funeral, some good friends and fellow parishioners lost a baby boy at nine months' gestation. The week after our daughters' Funeral Mass, we were all back in church for another baby funeral! Fr. Newman began his homily by sharing his initial reaction to God: "What are you doing?" Herein I saw the protective nature this pastor has for his flock. His reaction was not one of the "spiritualizers" C. S. Lewis speaks of, but of a man who wrestles with God. Not a man who doubts, but a man like Moses, who spoke honestly to God when interceding for his people. We often think of the term "pastor" as soft and gentle, but protecting your sheep is not always a soft and gentle work.

Perhaps the greatest pain of a father is seeing his children suffer. Herein, I have experienced the love of my own father in a unique and blessed way. I have never seen him as sad as when he held Abigail's beautiful but lifeless body, just days after having had his heart stolen by her when he met her in the PCICU. Yet his grief was not just at losing a granddaughter, but at seeing his son grief stricken. My mother told me that in nearly forty years of marriage she has never seen him this troubled. I am so grateful for his love and for being there for me during this time. It has visibly revealed to me the sorrow our heavenly Father feels when we grieve.

Finally, I have seen the pain in my Christian brothers. When we returned home to Greenville, I was particularly struck by one friend who greeted us after our first Mass back. He didn't have anything to say (what could he say?), but I could see the sorrow in his eyes. I then began to see this in my other brother's eyes. I knew that they had mourned and prayed.

Never have I been more grateful for the Fraternus brotherhood than since these tragedies. Men who scarcely knew me were praying, having Masses offered, and even sending gifts. Fraternus is a Catholic brotherhood with the mission of mentoring boys into virtuous men.

One of my Fraternus brothers interrupted his busy life and took off several days to travel and be at the funeral. When I thanked him, he simply remarked that this is what brothers do. Well stated. I am not in this alone, or even just with my family. God has blessed me with brothers who help carry this cross.

Through all of this, never have I so intensely longed for the next life. The separation from my daughters is like a piercing sword in my heart that twists itself back and forth a few times each day. I love my wife. I love my children here on earth. I don't want to be separated from them in any way, either. I cherish them more because of losing Chiara and Abigail. I enjoy my time with them, and especially with Bridget.

Yet my perspective has shifted. I have always believed in God and believed in heaven and hell. I have recited the Creed at Mass, during the Divine Office, and in the Rosary thousands of times . . . "I believe in the resurrection of the body and life everlasting." It is not as if I did not believe before. I did believe, but now I believe *and I long*. This longing often reaches its pinnacle at Sunday Mass. As we "lift up our hearts," my wife and I experience the bittersweet reality that we have joined the worship of heaven. We imagine Abigail and Chiara worshipping among the throngs of angels and saints. During Mass, we receive a foretaste of that perfect and glorious communion of love they already have with God and all the saints, and we rejoice with them. We are grateful for this mystical union, but rather than satisfy, it only intensifies our longing.

There is no glossing over it: death stings, and grief is now a part of our life. But why should we be surprised? Jesus promised crosses for those who follow him. In fact, it seems as if the closer people are to God, the more trials he allows them to experience. I am reminded of St. Teresa of Avila as she cried to God in a trial: "When wilt thou cease from scattering obstacles in our path?" "Do not complain, daughter," the Divine Master answered, "for it is ever thus that I treat my friends." "Ah, Lord, it is also on that account that thou hast so few!" This bit of slapstick saintly humor reveals a great truth: many shy from true religion out of fear it will be too hard.

There is no escaping it—if you seek to follow Jesus, you will know and share in his Cross in one way or another. All human beings know suffering, but for those of us who follow Christ, our suffering can be joined to Christ's and thereby find redemption through it. In taking on human existence, in becoming Jesus of Nazareth, God entered into his creation fully and completely, playing fair by going before us in suffering and death. God has experienced these most human realities, but even at that he does not desire our suffering. God allows it because it is the only way for us to be perfectly joined to him. And from an eternal perspective, the more we become like him, the happier we will be.

So as strange as it may sound, while we would do anything to have our Abigail and Chiara in our arms, we can take some comfort in knowing that God has actually loved us in this tragedy. As we proclaim during the Easter Vigil on Holy Saturday night, "O truly necessary sin of Adam, destroyed completely by the death of Christ. O happy fault that earned so great, so glorious a redeemer!" God does not cause evil, but he allows it to bring a great good out of it. We can truly say God has shown his favor more to us, and given us deeper evidence of our sonship in him, through the death of Chiara Luce in the womb and the unexpected death of Abigail Rose in the surgery room. Our lives will never be the same.

Friends who have lost children have told us that while the pain may not always be this sharp, it will never be healed in this life. It will always be there. But so will God's love—in his Word, in the sacraments, and in the sacred liturgy. And God's love will always be available for us in our marriage, in our family life, and in you, my brothers and sisters in Christ. It is this love that will carry us through, until that day when "he will wipe every tear from their eyes, and there shall be no more death or mourning" (Rv 21:4a).

7

Losing an Infant

More Than Crosses

Ben Boudreaux

My name is Ben. I have been married to my wife, Joy, for twenty years. After struggling with infertility for a few years, we now have fifteen children. Eight of the children had to stay in the NICU for the early part of their lives. Five of them have moved into the kingdom already. The first two children, Mary Joe and Henry, were miscarriages. Later, we had stillbirth twin boys, Eric and Adam. Our most recent loss, Ella Mary, was due to trisomy 18. My experience with her life is what I will be sharing.

During the pregnancy, my wife and I were told that something was not correct with the baby's formation. It couldn't be confirmed at the time, but we would have to consult with a specialist. While we were processing the shock of the news, I remember hearing the physician advise the specialist over the phone that whatever you do, don't offer amniocentesis as we were a Catholic couple and would not want to risk the harm to the baby. It was somewhat comforting to know that our doctor was helping to keep us in line with the Church.

My wife and I decided that if there was nothing that could be done for the baby, we didn't want to know the condition. Maybe we already feared the worst, but we didn't want the worst to be a reality yet. The doctor and the specialist could not understand our reasoning and multiple times told us that they had never had such a strange request. We were advised that our daughter had a chromosome issue. Honestly, I don't remember when they told us the condition was "incompatible with life." We assumed on our part that maybe it was Down syndrome.

The thought of Down syndrome was hard enough to deal with. The realization that my child would be disabled scared me and many others in the house. How could we give her the care she needed? In the end, not knowing the diagnosis was a blessing. Not knowing with any certainty (the doctors were not certain either, as their prognosis was at best 75 percent correct) left room for hope. We were still able to fall in love with our child and pray unceasingly, leaving room for God to work in her life while she was still here with us. We felt that we still had something we could do instead of giving up.

We reached out to all friends and family who we thought would be serious in praying for her. We started going to a weekly healing service held by a Catholic priest who visited our city once a week. We did this faithfully, and I can't remember missing any. We also heard of a Catholic nun, a mystic, an hour's drive from our house who "spoke to Papa." We went to see her for two visits. According to this mystic, Papa told her that the doctors had it wrong. They were too focused on her feet as a sign of the issue. We were still very concerned and scared, but there was some comfort in the hope that all would be okay. I could not think of anything else we could do for our child. All we could do was hope for a miracle.

As the pregnancy progressed, however, the doctors became less supportive of our decisions. We were continually being questioned why we didn't want to know all the details. Having the genetic testing seemed to be less of a hazard now, and they demanded that we get it done. After debating, we thought if the testing could help determine whether we needed to be at a specialized hospital for the birth, then it would be worth it. However, we again didn't want to know the results. We were told in the end we could deliver locally.

When the delivery time came, our struggles with the doctor continued; we no longer needed to see the specialist. The Catholic pro-life doctor we have seen since we were married seemed to become a stumbling block instead of helping us make a compassionate decision. In retrospect, maybe he acted this way because he knew the test results that we had chosen not to know. Luckily, most of the comments he made stayed between him and me, but this was very difficult to shoulder by myself. While contractions were coming, and it was close to time to push, Ella's heartbeat would lower to dangerous levels. My wife and I decided it would be safer for the baby to be delivered by a cesarean section. We advised the doctor of our decision, and he didn't seem to like it. As memory serves, I was in a one-on-one conversation with him. I don't remember if it was to sign papers or if Joy had to go to the bathroom, but he felt he needed to convince me to talk it over with Joy and try to change her mind. "Let nature take its course." "Why put your wife in harm's way anyway?"

I couldn't believe it. As hard as this was, why did I have to be confronted with these comments? I told the doctor that we were going through with the C-section. I couldn't help but think the C-section was the better, pro-life thing to do. I didn't want to lose my wife, but I couldn't think about exchanging her life for another. It seemed to be very little risk to my wife—I was just getting scare tactics of hemorrhaging, and so on. I wanted so much to argue, fuss, and fight. But I couldn't. I had to be strong. I needed this man to be able to safely deliver the baby and not kill my wife due to some emotional distress I had caused.

While I was dressing for the emergency room, the doctor found another chance to catch me alone. He wanted to make sure I knew this was bad medicine, and the baby was likely to die anyway. After a prayer he walked me into the room, so I had little time to get my bearings before joining my wife's side. My only hope was that my true emotions could hide behind the mask, knowing full well my eyes might deceive me.

As I entered the room, my wife of course asked immediately, "What's wrong?" I didn't know what to say or do but just shrugged. I couldn't talk because I feared my voice would crack. I was holding her hand, head, hair, or shoulder, you know, whatever they had left accessible for me. Despite all the doctor's warnings, the C-section was successful, and we were told it was a girl. Mixed with the happiness that she had arrived, I was waiting on pins and needles as it was about to get bad again. I was waiting for the shoe to drop. My wife's look of excitement would soon change because the doctor told me, "This won't end well." The foreboding news came. There was something wrong with the baby, and she would be moved to the NICU immediately. Her life was in jeopardy. I played out the whole operation in my head. I would be unable to protect her from the pain. There was nothing I could do. Joy was inconsolable, but we had to put our army boots back on again.

Instead of staying with my wife until she was at least sewn together, I had to leave and follow the nurses with Ella to a nearby holding area. I felt obligated to be with her. It wasn't clear to me if I felt obligated to be with Ella so that she didn't die without a parent near, or to be a witness to everything so that I could share the details with Joy later on. Mostly, I felt I couldn't do this.

We were thrown into a confusing fog pit of frustration. With the knowledge that Ella was alive for now but might not be for long, I felt the need to contact family and friends. I tried calling a few priests I knew personally for an emergency baptism. One was at a retreat, one at a movie, one on vacation states away. I turned it over to a person I knew I could count on, my brother Mark. He had recently rekindled his devotion to the Church, and it was easy to tell him, "I need a priest." I knew if anyone could get it done, he was going to be the fastest at it.

Close family and a priest arrived to have a baptism in the NICU. Ella was now a child of God. We had struggled with our stillbirth twins not being baptized. I guess you can say we felt prepared for Ella's passing as much as a parent could be. What was I feeling? What was I thinking? *We prayed so hard and did so much; she should not die! We deserve some time with her. Everything was supposed to be okay. Why would the prayers, consulting, and healing services be in vain?* Strange as it seemed, though, I still didn't think it was God's unfaithfulness or lack of mercy. It felt more like an inner struggle between my head and my heart. I always knew it was in his hands.

Days felt like weeks while Joy was recovering. Ella made it through the night, then another night, and another. She was living. After a few more specialist visits, we were told her condition was trisomy 18. It is not life-sustaining. Somehow, her heart had a hole in it, which is very common, but God's grace was on the good side. Instead of her blood being depleted of oxygen, the hole allowed her blood to provide oxygenation to her body. She was going to be able to come home!

Her life was still in jeopardy, but since there was nothing that could be done, she was released to hospice care. Doctors, nurses, and medical equipment invaded our house. The house was now an extension of the hospital and specialist offices. Visitors had to be limited.

We needed to learn what would keep Ella comfortable. We found through time that sunlight seemed to aggravate her condition. Her spine seemed to be in constant pain. Chiropractic adjustments brought some relief, but the drive home often undid the procedure. To prevent her discomfort, we started attending Mass in two shifts. We felt it in her best interests that we did not attend Mass as a family.

Acetaminophen was often administered around the clock. She seemed to always be in pain. When the acetaminophen started affecting her liver, we had to change to ibuprofen and eventually morphine. Her pain sometimes made us yell and scream, "God, take her now if she has to live like this!" She also struggled with constipation. We had to administer medicine to relieve her daily. I often felt a stranger or even invisible in my own home. Doctors knew what needed to be done. My wife did most of it. I was too afraid to hurt Ella. She was so fragile or at least seemed to be. I felt in the way and unable to help. I am certain I did feed her. The grief seems to have blocked the memory. I can't even remember Joy feeding her. Was it a bottle or tube? I cannot answer that. I remember diaper changes, maybe because we were looking for stool. I know I rocked her, but I can't remember any particular time. All this hurts me to this day as if I still feel I was inattentive to her presence. Did I even look her in the face? Did I talk to her? I remember her reaching for my beard, but I don't even know if I responded to her trying to get my attention. Maybe she was trying to console me. To this day, I keep a beard to remember her. I never kept a beard before her birth. I wonder at times if I would have the heart to shave it off completely.

She did love her baths, however. There seemed to be a relaxation in her face and her body when she was in the tub. It gave us breath and a sense of genuinely making a difference. The relief was short-lived as it hurt her again to get her dressed. I'm sure with her tiny frame getting warm wasn't easy either.

On Valentine's Day, Ella ended her day with a bath and lotion from Joy. She had just passed stool, had her medicines, and was comfortable and ready for bed. We held her for a little while, but she was so comfortable we decided to put her in her bed for the night. When Joy and I returned to our room later, Joy checked on her while I was in the bathroom. Joy found her dead. "Ben!" I ran to her side. I picked up Ella and couldn't stop crying. The moment we knew would come, were frequently reminded about, feared, dreaded, prayed for, prayed that it would never come, was here.

Strange as it may sound, we had the same thing happen—we couldn't find a priest. I had to call three different ones again before someone came. I called family over and had to reach out to the funeral home to come get the body. You know, the busy of the ugliness. To add insult to our pain, the coroner showed up to pick up Ella's body, not with a casket, not with a stretcher, but with a toolbox. It seemed so inhumane, such a lack of respect. Her body, her life, was not worth more? We couldn't even watch them take her away. Anger set in, and we expressed our disapproval and disgust, hoping no other family would have to endure that treatment.

Ella was born June 8, 2015, and died eight months and six days later on Valentine's Day of 2016. She was unable to speak. She was unable to socialize. She had very few visitors, but she had a prayer army. I could not believe my eyes when I saw so many people show up for her funeral. Three priests presided. Hundreds attended. I even had people drive across the state to meet us. How could she have touched so many lives?

She made a difference in so many lives by only carrying her cross.

As difficult as the miscarriages were, the stillbirths seemed to hit me harder, but child loss took the wind out of me. It's strange how the effect is different with each loss. Miscarriages seem to hit only the couple. The world doesn't recognize the loss. Everyone wants you just to forget the child, as well as the pregnancy. Stillbirths add a physical presence to the loss and affect close friends and family a little more, but you still get the comment "At least you didn't get to know them," as if that is any comfort. With child loss of any age, there is more widespread compassion. Granted, there are still some clueless people, which for me made the grief worse. As surprised as I was by the number of people showing up to Ella's funeral because her life touched them, it hurt when people I expected to show up didn't. The pain was even greater when others defended the person's actions and still do to this day. I have come to forgive, but forgetting is still hard, maybe because it was such a shock that couldn't be explained.

There came a time when I found some comfort in the chromosome issue. It reinforced that life is a miracle, and if the genes are not perfect, life is off balance. This knowledge made me believe that the miscarriages and stillbirths were somehow caused by the same thing. I have come to understand that even during the tragedies and the wondering why healing wasn't coming, Christ was with us. The conviction to attend healing Masses and to search out the mystic, to form a prayer army, to not want to know Ella's condition before birth so we could love her instead of giving up on her, to accept help from hospice, and many other actions that didn't seem to feel like I was in control—he was there in all of it. It seemed superhuman actions were flowing through me. Instead of blaming God, I was with him, and he was with me.

I still feel an unspoken bond with God stronger than before. I don't know why, but it sort of feels like meeting other fathers of loss.

No words need to be shared, experiences could be different, but that pain, that grief, that scar upon our souls connects us.

I heard a homily at Easter about the story of the road to Emmaus. The Spirit flowed through our priest to inspire me about "coming to know him in the breaking of the bread" (see Luke 24:35). As we all believe, the bread is Christ's Body. So, in essence, we come to know Christ through the breaking of his Body. Without meaning to be disrespectful, I think, to some extent, I have come to know Jesus through Ella's body breaking. Her pains. Her struggles. Her cross. Her effect on others. The morphine, laxatives, weak body, thin bones, crippled feet, pain-stricken face. Pain and suffering seem to be the love story and the means to come closer to God. Our "Why me?" questions seem to be answered every time more pain and struggle come: "Because I love you."

We have only two pictures of Ella in which she doesn't appear to be hurting. In one, she is reaching for my son's chin, reminding me of when she did the same to me. We also have a video of her where she seems to be talking to an angel that came to visit one day not long before she passed.

Over the years, we tried support groups to deal with the losses of our children; they just didn't seem to work for me. Granted, they took some part of the loneliness away, but maybe through my hardness of heart I couldn't accept that anyone could help me. No one's experience was going to be the same as mine, so how could they help? There were a few times we seemed to be the most experienced in the room with our number of losses. If someone were in the room with the same losses, I would likely have discounted them for not being the same age, financial status, or other social measure. I would judge them until they were not "relevant" to my needs. It's pretty sad, and I am not proud of those feelings. But let me tell you, I was wrong. It is becoming more pronounced in day-to-day conversations: "It's not about you." There's some comfort in that. Knowing someone else was also hurt reinforces that it wasn't just some luck of the draw or 1 in 100 billion odds. The grief seemed to force me into feeling inconsolable, isolated, and alone. But I couldn't continue like that. I would have to share my story with others. I was not looking for the same "process" of loss, but the "effects" of the loss. Be it the grief, growing past the hurt, or even the blessings. We need each other. If nothing else, just to know about each other.

Returning to public life was always hard. It seems everyone only asked about my wife. Guess I didn't matter or wasn't supposed to have feelings. How do I address my living children? Do I let them see me cry? Do I hide the tears in hopes of not scaring them? We are still trying to figure that out. In the meantime, we have pictures of the children we have lost on the wall, birthday cakes, and Christmas stockings in their names. We pray to them, our saints. As my mom always told me, those saints need something to do, and since we are their parents, we can tell them what to do.

Take heart, my friend. God is with us. As a priest once said, "Our crosses are more than crosses. They are crucifixes, as there is Jesus on them."

8

Losing a Young Child

The Third

W. Pat Bordes II

You are going to have a son, she said. I could hardly contain myself as the doctor told Jessica and me our baby was going to be a boy. I remember I could not wait to tell my dad he was going to have a grandson. God had already blessed us with a daughter, so this was going to be a perfect family in my mind—a girl and a boy.

I grew up thinking I wanted a family with four or five kids. I have always worked hard; I had my first job at fourteen years old and saved enough money to buy my first car at fifteen, before I even had my driver's license. After graduating high school, I went straight to college. At that point, I thought I would marry young and have lots of kids. I grew up Catholic and had what I would now call a lukewarm spiritual life but for the most part attended Mass and prayed regularly. I did pray that God would put someone in my life to marry. Looking back now, I see how blessed I have been all my life because God always answered my prayers. Most guys I knew in college were running from the very thing I was praying for. But I had a plan! And things were not going according to my plan.

I graduated college and got a job right away in New Orleans, Louisiana. I was having fun, going out, working hard, but could not find the person I was willing to spend the rest of my life with. I continued to pray and began visiting the adoration chapel, telling God that I was getting older, and that it was time if I wanted those four or five kids.

After a couple of job changes, I ended up working in Eunice, Louisiana. By this time, I had made it all the way to my mid-twenties. I had family in Eunice, and one day my cousin's good friend said she had a niece she wanted me to meet from Lake Charles. I met Jessica Bourgeois. She was kind and had a warm heart, and after about a year of dating, I knew she was the one. I remember going to Mom and Dad and telling them I was going to finally do it: I was going to ask Jessica to marry me; she was the one. They were so excited for me. At the time I was thinking, *God finally answered my prayers*, but, in retrospect, I see that God knew what he was doing all along. We got married when we were both twenty-nine years old. We both knew we wanted a family and should start right away.

On December 12, 1998, our daughter was born—Shelby Lynn. In our eyes, she was the most beautiful baby girl ever born. I was so excited about her and all she brought to our life. I spoke to Jessica about maybe trying one more time for a boy, and she agreed. On January 5, 2003, we were blessed with a boy, and I had my perfect family. God is so good to me. I vividly remember walking down the hallway in the hospital and opening the doors that led to the nursery and seeing my dad looking through the window at his newborn grandson. I could see a tear in his eye. I do not think until that point I had ever seen my dad cry. He turned and I looked him in the eyes, and we began to cry tears of joy together. We embraced with the biggest hug we've ever had, and I remember gasping for breath telling him, "Daddy, I just hope I can teach him half the things you have taught me and be half the man you are to me to my son." As if his birth wasn't enough excitement for us, our boy was the first baby born in 2003 in Acadia Parish. The newspaper took a photo and showered us with gifts they had collected from local businesses. What a proud moment when the picture appeared in the paper with my son's name across the top headline in bold—FIRST BABY OF 2003.

I was named after my dad; I was the second. I thought about naming my son the third but really liked the sound of Trey. I envisioned how it would sound screaming from the bleachers, "Watch the ball all the way in, Trey." I liked the way it sounded. Jessica agreed, so we named him Trey Patrick. Later Jessica found a black-and-white picture of my dad when he was a young boy, a picture of me around the same age, and one of Trey, and put them in matching frames. I was so proud to hang them on the wall. The pictures still hang there today.

One and a half years went by, and I was so thankful to God for my beautiful family. One Saturday, Jessica's aunt, the same aunt who introduced us, invited our daughter Shelby to sleep at her house for the night. So it was just Jessica, Trey, and me at home that night. I remember just as Jessica and I lay down in bed I could hear Trey's little footsteps running down the hall. He came into our room and ran up on my side and slammed his little body against the bed with a big smile and both arms stretched up, waiting for a hug. I reached down and hugged and kissed him. Then his little bitty footsteps went running around the bed with arms stretched high and a big smile for a hug and kiss from his mommy, and off he went running down the hall back to his bed.

The next morning, Sunday, September 14, 2004, I woke up and decided to go get us some donuts. I went down the stairs; Jessica was already in the kitchen. I told her where I was going and walked out the door. I remember backing up my truck and feeling and hearing a big thump. I remember cursing to myself, "Them damn kids next door left a damn bike in our driveway again." I threw it in park, flung open my door, and jumped out of my truck to go move the damn bike.

Oh my God . . . it was Trey lying on the cement. I ran screaming. I couldn't get to him fast enough. I ran over my own son! Jessica must have heard me from inside the house because she came running. She ran back inside to dial 911. With everything I had, I began blowing air into his mouth. I was pumping his chest and blowing air. Blood was coming out of his little nose and ears. I did not notice the big pool of blood all around me on the cement at the time. I was just pumping and blowing, pumping and blowing. I also did not notice my screaming; I was so loud the neighbors and members of the church down the road came and surrounded us. The first responders got there and physically moved me away and told me, "Let us work." The ambulance got there and left in an instant. My uncle heard the 911 dispatch on his neighbor's scanner and recognized the address and came right away. He told Jessica and me to get in the car; he would drive us to the hospital. The hospital was only about seven minutes away, but it was taking forever. I kept hollering at my uncle, "June, hurry, hurry up!" I remember beginning to pray out loud, yelling at God to save my son. I was negotiating, telling him all kinds of things I would do if he would just save my son.

They brought Jessica and me behind a curtained area in the emergency room to wait. Finally, the head ER doctor on duty came and sat calmly next to us and said, "I am so sorry, but your son did not make it." I yelled, "No! We need to keep working!" Then we walked to where Trey was. He was cleaned up and wrapped in a blanket. All I could see was his face. We went to him.

By this time, several family members were there in the room surrounding the bed and in the hallway. I remember screaming, "This can't be happening to me. Wake me up, dammit, I must be dreaming!" I remember yelling to my father-in-law, who had already made it from Lake Charles, "I can pick up this whole f---ing hospital right now, but I can't save my son!" I really at the time did not know what I was doing, but I began swinging my arms, knocking things down. They grabbed me and held me.

At some point, family began to slowly walk me out of the room. I remember seeing a doctor I knew in the room as we made our way out. I begged and pleaded with her, "Please, KK, do something, please save my son!" She began to cry and hugged me. Jessica's aunt brought Shelby to the hospital; it was no coincidence she was not at home this morning. I saw little Shelby, and she saw me. She looked up at me and with her innocent little voice said, "Daddy, you have to be careful." I wanted to die. How could God have done this to me?

The next few days were filled with all sorts of emotions, but mostly anger and despair. I can't quite explain it . . . I felt as if my body was there but inside of me was soaring somewhere else. I guess I just could not believe this was all really happening. I do remember Jessica and I held on to each other and would not let go. We just sat there mostly and could not let go of each other. I traveled to a place so deep inside of me I never knew it existed and had thoughts I didn't know were even possible for me to have.

When it came time for the funeral, it felt as though hundreds and hundreds of people came to the funeral home; it was daunting. I mostly cried. I remember later someone saying that was one of the saddest visits to the funeral home they had ever made. I do remember a cousin reaching down to where I was sitting and hugging me; he was a big, strong man. He hugged me tight and told me to take all the strength he had, and for some reason that gave me a little strength. Almost to every person who reached down to hug me, I just kept repeating, "What am I going to do?" The sheriff came, and I don't know where this came from, but I remember standing up and telling him loudly, "You finally made it. Handcuff me now and let me rot in jail! I killed my own son!" I knew him and he was just there to pay his respects, but at the time I had other ideas.

After the funeral, for a few days I didn't know how I was going to even put one foot in front of the other. We had so many people write us letters sharing either their story or condolences. We had many people stopping by with good intentions trying to give us encouragement. Some came to tell us about how they lost a loved one or child. My emotions were all over the place. I remember at one point someone brought me a tree to plant in the backyard. I guess I thought that was going to make me feel better. I started digging the hole and kept digging and digging and digging, faster and faster. I kept telling myself in a rage, *Right now I have the strength to dig a hole all the way to China, but I can't bring my son back.* When I snapped back into the present,

I looked down into the huge hole I had dug. I turned around and saw my dad at the window watching me. He was crying. Today, I realize the sorrow he must have felt at that moment to see his son in so much pain, and there was nothing he could do.

The love shown to us in the community—the letters and visits—really was comforting and did spark some sense of hope, although it didn't seem like it much at the time. This is when we first met Fr. Bill. I remember Jessica and I were sitting next to each other on the couch, and he walked into the room. My first thought was, *I don't want to hear no holy-rolly shit right now from you, priest.* The first thing he said was, "Y'all mind if we went outside so I can smoke a cigarette?" I had never before met a priest who smoked. We laughed about it for years afterward. He met us where we were, and we will always love him so much for it. God rest his soul.

Time would move on, and I read a few books people had given me about grieving. I learned there are a few stages in the grieving process with no progression from the first to the last step. It is a continuous weave between one stage and another, back and forth, and you move at your own pace. Jessica and I both came to understand that and tried to give each other the space we needed and tried to be patient with each other as we were rarely on the same page. At one point, she wanted to put a photo in every corner of the house to remember Trey, but for me it was just too painful. I did not want any pictures of him at all, anywhere. It was difficult, but we got through it with help.

I am pretty headstrong and never envisioned myself getting in a circle and sharing my feelings, but Jessica asked me to go with her to a nondenominational group meeting called Compassionate Friends. This was the only group meeting at the time for parents who lost children, and I am glad I went. It helped me to know that many others had lost children, I was not the only one, and they could somewhat relate. They did not pretend to know "exactly what you are going through," but all shared a similar story. We also took Shelby to a place called Healing House. It was a place for siblings to share their feelings with other siblings about their losses.

It was over a year now and I was still struggling with God, and every now and then I had moments of uncontrollable emotions rising to the surface. I remember we were shopping in Sears one day, and down one of the aisles an overwhelming feeling of despair came over me. "Did I really back over my son? Is this real? Where am I? This is so unbelievable!" As I began to shed tears, Jessica realized what was happening and grabbed my wrist and squeezed it tight. This snapped me back to the present. Another time I was tailgating before my beloved Ragin' Cajuns football game, watching the young boys who were there throwing the football to each other. This same feeling came over me, and it was overwhelming. I would never see my son throw a football. I began to cry. The friend standing next to me was stunned. All he could do was look at me with sorrow because this kind of grief comes from so deep within and was unlike anything he had ever experienced. He just stared at me, wanting to help me; all I could say was, "My son." These episodes came further and further apart, but I knew I needed something.

I had reached what I describe as a fork in the journey of my life. At this point I felt I had two choices: one was to go down a wide and easy, feel-good road of self-destruction and desolation; the other was to go down the much harder, narrower, and deeper road of suffering, sacrifice, and redemption.

One day the doorbell rang, and standing at the door was a person I knew but had never formally met. He was the mayor pro tempore of our city. He was a little older than me and someone I admired. I knew him to be a spiritual man and a man of conviction. After a few minutes of small talk, he told me he was part of a small group of men, a spiritual group, who met once a week. He told me each of their names, and I knew all of them. He said as a group they decided one of them should come talk to me, see how I was doing, and tell me about Cursillo. He said he immediately volunteered. He asked me if I had ever heard of Cursillo. I told him I knew it was some kind of retreat but didn't know anything else about it. He said if I ever wanted to go, he would sponsor me.

I felt that this might be that something that I needed. So I made up my mind and made my Cursillo in February 2005, about a year and five months after Trey's death. The most profound thing I learned at Cursillo was that God did love me. And I learned how to have a deep and personal relationship with my Lord and Savior Jesus Christ. Jesus did not promise there would be no hardships in life. Look at what he went through to prove it. He did, however, promise that if you put all your trust in him, he will be there with you no matter what the circumstances. He promised that when your cross becomes heavy, he will carry you through it. This is the hope that I cling to. Every morning I wake up, get out of bed, and lovingly pick up my cross, because I know that is what will redeem me. It is my hope that this day someone, through my cross, will see him who dwells in me, Christ, Our Lord. I know his grace is sufficient and, by my persisting in the sacraments he gave us, I will find the peace and joy I long for.

I became a part of that spiritual group of local men who reached out to me. I continue to meet with my spiritual brothers once a week after all these years. I am not sure where I would be today without them.

Long ago, I shut the door, locked it, and threw away the key to that dark place inside of me. I went back to that place to share my experience with you. I went there with you in the hope that the sight of me lovingly and sacrificially carrying my cross will give hope to you who may be suffering at this very moment. After all these years of my continuous journey, it is the trust I have put in God and the knowledge that his mercy and love for me are endless, and a deep and growing relationship with Jesus Christ, that will sustain me for the rest of my life.

God bless you.

9

Losing a Young Child

Radical Acceptance

Ryan Breaux

I met Kelly at a bar in 1999 on Mardi Gras. It only took two weeks of dating for me to fall head over heels in love with her and utter the words, "I love you." She was different and super fun. Marriage began to cross my mind. I could picture my life with her. We dated for three and a half years and married on July 13, 2002, at our home parish, St. Bernard Catholic Church, in Breaux Bridge, Louisiana, where I had received every sacrament.

Life seemed to be going pretty well. I had a beautiful wife who supported my dirt bike racing, a good job, and a great family. But suffering came early on for us. After only seven months of marriage, I wrecked my dirt bike and broke my back. I hit a jump and landed on a 55-gallon drum, which sent me into the air and then crashing down headfirst. I shattered my T3 and T5 vertebrae; my T4 was dislodged. For a time, I was paralyzed. I had spinal surgery and recovered, but this was the first of many sufferings that our family was going to endure; I just didn't know yet.

I think the dirt bike accident was when my conversion back to the Church really happened. My life flashed before my eyes during this time, and the reality that I could so easily have died in that accident made me think about what I wanted in life. Kelly and I always wanted children and were open to life since the start of our marriage. The reality eighteen months later was that we hadn't conceived. This made us question if something was going on with our fertility that we might need to have checked.

We were shocked to find out that we were among those couples who couldn't conceive on demand. It took years of prayers, tears, and emotional roller coasters for both of us. It was a large cross to bear at the time, especially as we watched our friends getting pregnant and having babies. We were emotionally and financially invested. Conceiving became an obsession each month. Tracking, charting, and figuring out what was going on inside my wife's body was very scary.

Finally, after four rounds of fertility shots,[1] Kelly was pregnant. When we went in for the ultrasound, two tiny sacks popped up on the screen. Twins! We were over the moon and felt this was a huge blessing, a two-for-one deal! Everything went as planned until Kelly was about seventeen weeks pregnant, and the high-risk doctor told us that there was a possibility that one of our babies, Emma Grace, might have something genetically abnormal. We refused all tests because of the risks involved. We even told the doctor, "God wouldn't give us more than we can handle." Ironically, what happened was more than we could handle, but at the time, we trusted God.

October 16, 2005, was the scariest and happiest day of my life, second to marrying Kelly. Kelly had a placental abruption at twenty-eight weeks, and the babies had to be removed immediately. Talon arrived at 1:28 p.m., weighing 3 pounds, 1 ounce; and Emma Grace arrived at 1:29 p.m., weighing 2 pounds, 5 ounces. The babies were tiny and had to be rushed to the NICU and placed on ventilators. The events rolled by so quickly that we really don't remember the play-by-play. We woke up the next morning to five doctors in our room with an update. This was not good.

The doctors were confident that Talon had trisomy 21, or Down syndrome. It was confirmed on day ten with a positive genetic test. We could live with this. We could survive this. As long as the babies were healthy and lived, we could deal with this. But things weren't okay, and the babies weren't healthy. They were tiny and needed a lot of support and medical attention. Things began to deteriorate on day thirteen for Talon, and on October 31, Kelly called me in a panic with the words, "Talon is dying." I was an hour away, and I took off for the hospital. I prayed the whole way.

When I arrived, Kelly was distraught. Talon was lying in the Isolette, swollen and bruised. It looked like death was near. I managed to gather all the strength I had in my body and just hold my wife as she melted into a puddle of sobs. We knew that we needed to get a priest to baptize him, but after contacting our parish with no luck, we allowed the hospital to contact a sweet nun. She came immediately.

As we watched her pray over his tiny body and say those words, "I baptize you in the name of the Father, and the Son, and the Holy Spirit," we sobbed. At that moment, Talon became God's. Later that night, we watched him take his last breath, crossing over to heaven for eternity.

Just like when Jesus was taken down from the Cross, the nurses placed Talon's tiny lifeless body into Kelly's arms, then mine. Holding my dead son in my arms was devastating. All the dreams of playing catch, kicking a soccer ball, teaching him how to fix a flat tire were gone. It felt incredibly hard to breathe. I left the NICU that night with a shattered heart; it felt like a million tiny pieces that could never be put back together again.

Burying Talon was extremely difficult for our entire family. He was just fifteen days old. His casket was so small and light that I carried it alone, sobbing. We had never thought this could happen to us. How could this be our story?

At this point, Kelly and I were struggling with our faith silently. It was one of those talks that never really happened. We could only take the struggle day by day.

On the day we buried Talon, we found out Emma Grace had an infection too. We were enraged. Through the process of watching Talon fight for his life, we never found out the type of infection he had until the day we buried him. It was a slap in the face to find out after your child has died what he died from. Pseudomonas sepsis claimed my son's life.

Emma Grace's infection was different. She had MRSA staph. This caused her to have a mycotic clot in the right atrium of her heart and three aneurysms in her vascular system. She needed the aneurysms repaired because if they ruptured, she, too, would be facing death. But where would we go to have the surgery? Four out of the five leading pediatric cardiothoracic surgeons said she would die in surgery. This left one option—Cook Children's Medical Center in Fort Worth, Texas. The jet came to get us at the airport, and Emma Grace was transported for surgery.

By the grace of God, Emma Grace made it through the eight-hour surgery, and she was able to return home after two and a half weeks. Once home, we tried to wean her off the oxygen therapy, but her blood oxygen would drop dangerously low. She could not let go of the 1/4 liter of oxygen. Once Emma hit the 4 pound, 4 ounce mark, the doctors scheduled a round of tests and an overnight stay for us to learn how to care for her.

Kelly arrived at the hospital to spend the night while I was at work. As the nurses were setting up the room, they went over how to use the equipment and left. It was up to Kelly to follow the schedule, with a nurse checking in on Emma Grace every once in a while. My sister stopped in on her lunch break while Kelly was holding Emma Grace and noticed that our daughter was breathing funny. She called in the nurse, who checked the equipment and discovered that the oxygen tank had come unplugged. Kelly began to weep beyond consoling and told my sister, "I can't do this." Fear and anxiety set in, and Kelly had a panic attack. The anxiety was so massive that she started to throw up.

My sister called me, and I rushed over to the hospital. Kelly could not stop throwing up and felt the urge to sleep. She slept on and off for forty-eight hours. The reality that Emma Grace could die on her watch was more than she could handle. I managed to learn everything and take over. My wife was so scared, and it was heartbreaking to watch.

On January 9, 2006, three days after the twins' due date, Emma Grace was released to go home. Her homecoming was mixed with joy and fear and was really overwhelming for my wife. I tried my best to be attentive to her, but she couldn't handle the stress and pressure of medical attention needed for Emma Grace. The first week Emma was home, Kelly lost eleven pounds. I watched her as she struggled to eat and sleep; just waking to face the day was hard for her. I did not understand what was going on inside of my wife's body. I struggled to know what to say or do. I just couldn't watch my wife go through this any longer, so I called my sister, who worked at our OB's office, to talk about what we could do. We never thought about a delayed reaction to grief or the stages of grief.

The bills from the hospital were astronomical. I was working, but Kelly couldn't. She became Emma Grace's primary caregiver, and we were down to one income. After a couple of months, it wasn't just the grief that was compounding; it was all of the stressors rolled up into one package that we tried to manage while taking care of Emma. I was despondent and terrified for our family.

Kelly reluctantly went to counseling, as suggested by her doctor and lovingly persuaded by me. She was afraid the grief of losing Talon and the stress of Emma Grace's care could have triggered bipolar disorder, a condition her mother had that is genetic and usually triggered by a stressful or traumatic situation. Through this time, I watched the life leave Kelly's body. She stopped smiling and could barely manage the day-to-day. With the help of counseling and medication, she cared for Emma Grace and herself in their daily needs.

I would have liked to see her continue therapy, but after three sessions, she returned home and told me she wasn't going back. The counselor had not lost a child and, in the discussion, compared her own divorce to death. Kelly didn't take this comment well and told the counselor that she couldn't help her. I couldn't argue with her after what happened, and we tried to manage on our own.

Like too many men, I buried my pain and grief in my heart because I had to be strong for my wife. I wouldn't cry in front of her, because

I assumed that it would ruin her day if, by chance, she was having a decent one. Most days, crying all the way to work and all the way home was my reality. But I never shared my pain with Kelly. This formed a massive wedge within the walls of our home because more than ever Kelly needed someone to talk to. It was my job to be that person. I was the only one who understood what she was going through. I don't know why I felt that she didn't need to talk about it.

All of these marital struggles were occurring while we were trying to get Emma healthy. Around the time that Emma was two years old, we found out that we were expecting again. We also found out that Emma was going to need another surgery to correct a growth issue in her right leg from the surgery she underwent when she was five weeks old.

Kelly struggled with the timing of this gift of new life. She felt guilt knowing that just when Emma Grace was going to need her the most, she would be busy caring for another baby. Yet we embraced this pregnancy. Although it was thankfully uneventful, Kelly was still suffering from the post-traumatic stress of early prematurity and chromosome complication; added to that was the stress of planning for Emma Grace's upcoming surgery. On January 6, 2009, Estelle Gabriella was born—a healthy 7 pound, 9 ounce baby girl. She was so precious, and Emma adored her baby sister.

Later that year, we packed up the girls and headed to Florida for Emma Grace's surgery on July 24. Everything went according to plan, but within a few hours of surgery, Emma started to have multiple febrile seizures, which are seizures in children caused by fever. The surgery team had to intubate her to give her anti-seizure medication.

On July 26, Emma woke and asked her mother with the sweetest look on her face, as she did every morning, "Mommy, where are we going today?" Kelly said, "Sis, we aren't going anywhere, we are staying here today." She closed her eyes, saying, "OK," then opened them back up, looked directly into Kelly's eyes, and told her, "Mommy, I love you so much." It was like she pierced our soul with her words. That was the last time we ever heard our sweet girl speak.

Things went wrong very quickly after that. The medical team confirmed an H1N1 swine flu diagnosis, and within a few days, we had to make a decision. There was no way Emma would survive at this hospital with the care they could provide, so we moved her to Miami Children's Hospital and placed her on ECMO (extracorporeal membrane oxygenation), where a machine pumps and oxygenates a patient's blood outside the body, allowing the heart and lungs to rest.

It was an emotional roller coaster. Emma Grace had good days and bad days. There were times when we thought that she would be able to get off the machine, but like a vengeance, she would get another infection. Days turned into weeks, weeks turned into a month, and after seven and a half weeks of praying, consulting with doctors, and trying to make sense of it all, we just didn't know what else to do. Emma was making only tiny improvements, narrowing her chances of survival as the days went by.

On September 10, 2009, at 1:00 a.m., the phone rang. It was the on-call doctor, telling us something horrible had happened. A complication from the ECMO machine had left Emma's body barely receiving adequate oxygen. She was alive but very unstable. Her body was shutting down.

We literally ran to the car and jumped in. Running through the hospital and to the PICU seemed like the longest journey we had ever made. As we entered the PICU, we could hear her nurses praying over Emma from the hallway. I stood there for a second, scared to walk in as I watched them pray fiercely for our sweet girl as they worked on her. When we saw her, Kelly's knees buckled, and I caught her as she almost fainted. We started begging God. *God, why her? . . . Why again? . . . Why not me?* This was the longest day of our lives, watching her die. The staff tried everything to save our little girl. Kelly's crying was agony to my ears. As Emma Grace wailed off and on all day in pain, I cried silently, begging and pleading with God not to take her, but he didn't heal her. Emma Grace's heart kept stopping. The nurses tried everything possible to restart it.

Next came the hardest thing that I ever had to do in my life. With the nurses saying that there was nothing left for them to do, we had to decide whether to withdraw life support. Kelly and I embraced each other near the nurses' desk and just cried, holding each other. She looked up to me and said, "Ryan, I can't do that, I can't even say it out loud." Her body was trembling between the agonizing crying and sporadic breaths. That's when I had to make the decision that no parent ever wants to make.

Because we had signed the waivers to intervene in all life-saving measures, the nurses had to continue until the family withdrew support. By law, they could not turn off the machine; it had to be our call. Emma Grace's body was so battered and beaten from their attempts to restart her heart. I knew inside there was nothing more that could be done. As hard as it was, I knew it was my job as her father to do this. That is when I was forced to physically turn off the machine that was keeping my beautiful Emma's blood oxygenated. All the machines started alarming, and we saw a flat line on the screen. Her heart had stopped.

At approximately 7:30 p.m., for the second time in my life, one of my children died right before my eyes. They cleaned her off and placed her in Kelly's arms. Like Mary in the pietà holding her son's lifeless body, I saw a living pietà of my wife holding my daughter's lifeless body. This image remains painfully burned into my mind.

It's tough to remember all of the details about what happened that night. But one thing that I can tell you is that I pray never to have to make that decision again. I miss Emma so much that it hurts! I will also tell you this: the hurt will never go away. With time, we learn to deal with these waves of emotions triggered by the memories of the children we have lost.

A feeling of hopelessness came over me as I watched my wife process her anger with God. As we walked into the elevator, she let God have it. "I never thought this was going to happen to our family, not once, but twice. This is too much! God, where are you? Why are you ignoring our prayers?" Kelly screamed and shouted; I cried silently and embraced her as she melted to the floor. It was just too much for her, and I watched her shut down. When we got back to the apartment, I had to bathe my wife as she sat in the tub crying with a blank stare. She barely spoke, just cried. I even blow-dried her hair and tucked her into bed.

Burying Emma was very hard. We had memories that we tried to hold on to. All I could do was be healthy for Kelly. It was heart-wrenching to watch her suffer. The order is not how God designed it to be. Children are supposed to bury their parents and not vice versa. I tried to give Kelly the time and space to grieve. I put my grief on the back shelf so that we, as a family, could get through this darkness.

Our priest came over to our home to talk with us, and one of the things he told us was, "Wow, you have two little saints in heaven." Kelly wasn't pleased with this statement because most people don't tell you what having a little saint in heaven looks like. Here's the reality of having a little saint in heaven: You watch the life leave your child. You watch the nurses prepare her body so that you can hold your child while she is still warm and not hard, cold, and blue. Then you let someone take your child to the morgue, away from you, while you go back home and try your hardest to plan a funeral. It's kissing and hugging people and having to comfort them when they should be comforting you. Get ready, because soon they will shut the casket and you will never get to see your child's face again, ever. As your child's body passes through the church doors, you wish this was her wedding day, not her funeral. You wish you were walking her down the aisle, not grieving with her casket. Then they dig a hole in the ground, place her small coffin in the hole, and cover that hole with dirt. You leave the cemetery, and you go home without your child, whom you will never see again until heaven. That is what it's like to have a little saint in heaven.

Having a saint in heaven did not bring us comfort at first. But while we were getting the pictures together for Emma Grace's funeral, Kelly's friend noticed that Emma died on her baptism date, and thinking further, we realized that so did Talon. As time went on, we started to reflect on that, and it gradually sank in that both Talon and Emma had passed away on their baptismal dates. This must have meant something significant, but the pain was just too raw at that time to understand that significance.

I prayed nonstop for my family, especially for Kelly, but what I did wrong was pray alone. I never told my wife I was praying for her, or asked her to pray with me, or included her in my daily prayers. I didn't talk with her about what she was going through, and we found ourselves grieving separately and not together. It put a huge wedge in our marriage that should never have been there. I loved my wife with all of my heart, but I didn't know how to grieve the first time, much less this time.

Men, I need you to listen carefully: communication is critical. Not talking put an invisible wall between Kelly and me. Instead of yoking ourselves and grieving together, we were grieving separately.

Although I wanted to be Kelly's emotional rock, she needed a spiritual rock more. She needed someone to pray with, someone to talk with, someone to take her to church, someone to take her to adoration. I thought I was being healthy and helping, but I wasn't doing enough. We didn't ask for this cross. We didn't make a choice that led us here. It was out of our control. Instead of us facing this together, we tried to do it internally, silently, alone. And we were suffering so much. Kelly was in severe depression. Each night I would wipe tears from her face as they soaked her pillow.

There were many times when I was ready to do something without Kelly, like going fishing for the weekend or playing a football game with my friends. But she was just not ready for me to leave her alone. Wells of emotions would erupt within her at the idea, and I didn't understand why. Sometimes her emotion was anger (How could you even want to leave me? were her words), and often I would get angry back at her for not understanding my needs.

I needed some time away, but Kelly didn't understand because she was alone with a baby all week while I worked. So, when I came home, she needed a break. She needed me physically and emotionally. On the weekends, she didn't want to be alone, and her motivation wasn't selfish. She was just so broken inside and so depressed. Kelly felt she couldn't get through her grief without me. She needed me so very much and didn't know how to say this. She was afraid that if she said the words out loud, it would confirm how fragile and weak she really was. I was trying to be healthy for our family, in the fatherly role, but I was clueless about how to help her out of the darkness.

Kelly felt very weak and childlike most days, curled up in a ball in bed crying out in agony and pain. To be honest, most days she would cry not to be alone because she was afraid of the silence. It was so painful for her to go through this. I didn't know how to feel and would try to avoid my thoughts by staying busy.

Watching Kelly struggle so much with her grief and not knowing how to help her hit me to the core. I was the man of the house, but my broken heart prevented me from finding solutions. The only suggestion I had at the time was counseling, and Kelly resisted because of her previous experience after losing Talon. Our friends tried their best to invite us to do things, to get us out of the house. But most of these Saturday night outings included drinking. And as fun as it was those few times we went, I realized that Kelly would often drink too much. She was trying to numb the pain. While we were out, for that one night I saw a real smile on her face, so I didn't overthink it. But then like clockwork, the overindulgence in alcohol would leave her crying in bed all day Sunday, intensifying her pain. She would always apologize to me, feeling horrible for the mess she was left in. Sometimes we would talk, and it was good, but other times she got so angry at me for not understanding how she felt.

Three years after we lost Emma Grace, we found ourselves expecting again. It was an incredible blessing to our family because we wanted more children. Everything was fine until the day of Kelly's eleven-week checkup; the ultrasound tech searched and searched until she uttered the words, "There is no heartbeat." My poor wife was alone with the ultrasound tech and my sister. My sister called me to hurry to the doctor's office.

As I watched my wife crumble on the table in agony over the loss of another child, I held her and prayed silently. *Lord, why can't we have a healthy pregnancy? We just want babies, Lord. We promise to love them and to raise them to love you. Please send us a healthy baby, Lord.* We cried and cried and cried. We were both devastated. When the doctor met with us, Kelly told her that she was secretly waiting for this to happen. Like she knew it would end in another loss. Was this our life, our story? Just tragedy after tragedy? The suffering was intense.

When we made our way back home, I was so distraught watching Kelly scream and mourn the loss of another baby that I said I was going to get a vasectomy. And as I talked, she just listened. When I was done, she whispered, "No, we cannot make it permanent. We have to wait and trust that maybe we will conceive again." But that was six years ago, and we haven't conceived again.

Every time I mustered the courage to go back to church, Kelly would see babies or children who reminded her of Emma and Talon, or have flashbacks of the caskets down the aisle. She would cry the entire Mass or leave and go to the bathroom. She couldn't make it through Mass most Sundays. Soon enough we missed one week, then another, then four years passed. In 2013, when we enrolled Estelle in pre-kindergarten at our parish's school, Kelly became open to going back to church. She would go to Mass at school with Estelle on Thursdays because she would cry for her mom to go. This was the first step going back, but we did not go to Mass every Sunday as a family.

As angry as she was, I never thought my wife would be the one to bring me back to church. But in 2016, after a friend's child died, Kelly began a healing journey. First, trying to walk with her friend, she realized they were grieving differently. She joined her friend's prayer group, ended up going to RCIA for Confirmation, and was invited to make a Cursillo retreat. Kelly left the Cursillo retreat center in sanctifying grace. She was floating when she returned home, and I could tell that God had healed her. For the first time in years, I saw joy in my wife's eyes.

As much as I prayed that God would heal my wife, I never thought he would use my wife to get to me. But as I watched her transform into a holy woman after God's heart, I realized just what had happened to Kelly. For the first time in her life, she had been touched and amazingly healed by God. God made her broken, shattered heart into something so beautiful that it's hard for me to take my eyes off her. So instead, I started to grab her arm, and we stared at God together. When I saw her transforming and healing, I realized that I needed this as well. She was slowly helping me to soften my heart.

Kelly's conversion started when she went to Confession, was confirmed, and then attended Cursillo. It dawned on both of us that she was healed through the sacraments. At a men's conference, I went to Confession for the first time since our wedding vows. Kelly and I were now both in sanctifying grace and began to see our marriage transforming before our eyes. We knew we could find holiness within our marriage and started going to Confession as a family every month. The floodgates of grace were being opened. When you both have your eyes on God, the closer you get to him, the closer you get to each other. The following Pentecost, I attended a Cursillo retreat, and it was incredibly beautiful. I highly encourage you and your spouse to attend a retreat that will allow you to learn how to use the faith tools the Cursillo movement offers and that you can keep in your faith toolbox.

Since the retreat, I feel less stressed, am more relaxed in handling situations at work, am a better husband and father, and genuinely enjoy doing things for our church. And now, I genuinely feel that I am more in love with my wife because of our wounds than I was without them. I cherish her, and I cherish the cross that Jesus has given to us. With our cross, we were able to unite to his Cross and receive the graces that he died for us to have. I am so proud of how far my wife has come and the impact she has made on our family. It was truly needed, and we thank God every day.

We have learned that when we unite ourselves with the Cross and enter into Jesus's suffering with our own crosses, so much grace is poured out on us. We experience redemptive suffering. When we unite our suffering to the Cross of Christ, the whole world can see what love is. Our suffering is our witness; it gives others hope. To teach about suffering and to inspire others, we have to live it. Whereas many tend to isolate in their suffering, we have to be willing to show our wounds to others.

Today, after losing Talon and Emma Grace, Kelly and I look very differently at trials and tribulations. We have to see death beyond the Cross, even beyond the Resurrection. We have to look all the way to Pentecost and the Ascension, because that's when the story of our healing as individuals and as a couple occurred.

If God can bring us to this, he will bring us through it. Psalm 23 says, "Even though I walk through the valley of the shadow of death, I will fear no evil" (v. 4). So many times, God is asking us to walk through those valleys. At the time, we don't see the top of the mountain, because we have yet to climb the mountain. But if we are willing to start climbing, we will eventually see his glory. Every step we take is a struggle, but it's the only way to the top.

God has transformed our hearts and our marriage. And he desires that for you too. Will you let him? Will you let him be the King of your house? Will you let God be the center of your marriage? The only way you both will grow in holiness is if you do this together.

10

Losing a Preteen or Teenaged Child

Because of Griffin

Kevin LeBlanc

There's a picture of the two of us sitting on a sand dune in the Florida panhandle. The photo was taken from behind us, him and me, sitting with our legs bent and elbows on our knees, both looking to the left, both wearing baseball caps. When I look at that picture, when anyone looks at that picture, there is no doubt he is my son. While I could never compare the love I have for my two daughters and one son, Griffin, there is something special about the bond between a father and son, and my relationship with Griffin was no different. We laughed together, we played together, we cried together—we did everything together. In fact, my best friend was an eleven-year-old boy with a heart of gold and a wicked sense of humor, who was fiercely loyal and full of love. And on one Saturday in 2017 he was gone, and so were his laughs, his hugs, and his heart.

It was Labor Day weekend, and my entire family was spending the holiday at Big Lake, just south of Lake Charles, Louisiana. The fish weren't biting that day, so I remember the start of the day being pretty lazy. Later in the afternoon, my girls and my two nieces, along with their friends, wanted to go tubing on the lake. We loaded up the boat and the WaveRunner and headed out for an afternoon of fun. I was driving the boat with my wife, and my sister and her husband were riding with us as the girls rode on the tube behind the boat. Griffin and a friend were right behind the tube, snaking across the wake back and forth on the WaveRunners. As we were coming to a stop, I remember Griffin jumping the wake just as a boat was coming up. Now, they call it Big Lake for a reason: it's big, and this was the only other boat on the water that afternoon. My brother-in-law could see that the driver of the boat didn't see Griffin. We frantically waved for him to stop, but it was too late. We witnessed the unimaginable—Griffin's WaveRunner colliding with the front of the oncoming boat. The impact was so great that it blew Griffin out of his life jacket, and he went under the water.

The moment was surreal and I froze, as if my mind was not capable of believing what my eyes had just seen. Then I punched the throttle and raced toward the spot where I thought Griffin would have entered the water. My wife and I both jumped in, me without a life jacket, and I started diving the eight to ten feet from top to bottom, frantically waving my hands around the murky water trying to feel something. It all happened so fast. The first real feeling I remember having was exhaustion after five or six dives to the bottom searching for him.

When I made the last dive that I had the strength to make, I found myself halfway between the surface and the lake bottom, and I knew it had been too long and it was too late. For a split second, the thought came to me to just let go and to go meet him, but instead I began screaming Hail Marys while still under the water. As my head popped out of the water, the Hail Marys only got louder as my wife joined in. Someone threw me a life jacket, and I could see my wife thirty yards away, in the water, still calling for her baby. By now it had been twenty minutes or so since the accident, and I knew he had been underwater too long. I swam over to her and grabbed her face and told her he was gone—that's when I remember crying tears for the first time, tears that to this day still flow from time to time. The difference in the tears from then to now is that in that water, and for months after, the tears were from unbridled sorrow, pain that I had never known before, a sense of lonesomeness that I didn't know was possible. Today, when I am overwhelmed with tears about Griffin, more times than not, they are tears of gratitude for how big our God truly is.

Griffin's funeral was overwhelming. The church overflowed with people. I remember the smell of the incense and the sound of the music. Our parish priest crafted a homily that was so perfect, I still occasionally listen to it today. He quoted Hebrews 13:14 and said that we haven't here a lasting city and that we were made for more than this world. At the time, I had no idea what he was talking about. Today, I understand it perfectly. There are many words to describe the feelings that were swirling through my body the next days and months—numbness, brokenness, anger, confusion, loneliness, and what felt like fear.

C. S. Lewis said it best in his book *A Grief Observed*. He said grief was like an invisible blanket between him and the rest of the world, that he needed people to be around him but he wished they would talk to themselves. And we were blessed with so many people that put their lives on hold for us . . . and for months! There were always people in our house waiting on us, serving us. Friends still comment on what a beautiful example of service they witnessed during that time. For the most part, I just felt foggy, loopy, beaten, and hurt, as if my mind couldn't figure out how to work correctly, as if every day was some sort of alternate life and that none of it was real. I didn't want to go to sleep at night because I didn't want to see the accident in my dreams, and I didn't want to wake up in the morning because I didn't want it to be real. But most of all, I spent my days and nights wrestling with God, wrestling with believing and having faith in the providence of a God who could allow my son to be taken from me.

Just five short months before Griffin's death, I had a profound encounter with Our Lord at a Catholic retreat sitting outside at a camp in Grand Isle, Louisiana. You see, my faith wasn't always where it is today. For years I drifted away from the Church, away from the sacraments that would one day give me all the grace and peace I would need to survive this devastation. I sat outside at that camp, talking to God and going through the first examination of conscience I had ever attempted. Nineteen years had passed since my last Confession, and my relationship with Jesus Christ was nonexistent. During that examination, in a moment of complete vulnerability, the Holy Spirit blew through me, and I felt God tell me that he had forgiven me for everything I had ever done. I went straight to Confession and left feeling freer than I had ever felt in my life. When I got home, my life changed. Daily Mass, monthly (and sometimes weekly) Confession, fellowship with Catholic brothers, and accountability all became a working part of my life. In short, I dove back into the Catholic faith with the fervor of a new convert.

Five months later, my son died. I spent weeks asking God why and questioning my faith and the Church, but we were surrounded with holy people who answered our questions in the most spiritually mature manner. I remember a family meeting with our parish priest just days after the accident. I was a mess and cried through the entire visit. At one point, I turned to him and asked if he thought Griffin was looking down on me, seeing my misery and sadness and wanting to be back here with me. Our priest gave me an answer that, at the time, made me want to walk out of his office. He asked what made me think that Griffin would want to be back here with me when he was in everlasting bliss for eternity with his real Father. I thank God for that answer. I needed to hear that. I needed to believe that. I know today that our children are on loan to us and that they belong to an all-loving Father who loves and cares for them (for us) in ways we cannot comprehend.

But his answer presented another dilemma in my mind. I could accept that Griffin was with his heavenly Father, staring into the eyes of the Lamb of God each and every day in heaven. But where, and what, was heaven? Up until then, I never thought much about heaven. Newly back to the faith, relatively young, with a life to live, and still barely formed in the teachings of our faith, I knew nothing about heaven. And so, I read. I read every book I could get my hands on that had anything to do with heaven and near-death experiences. I learned so much about eternity from those accounts, but I still questioned where Griffin was. That's when God moved me for the second time in only a year.

I stayed away from work for several months until the fog began to lift. That's when I received a call from someone I had worked with on and off for ten years. She asked if I wanted to go back to work. I felt it was time—honestly, I thought work would be a distraction for me. I met her at the jobsite, and we began to talk about our faith and love for Jesus. During all those years of knowing her, I hadn't known she was Catholic, or even faithful for that matter. She spoke wisdom during our two-hour visit, and my heart began to open and soften. At the end of the job, she approached me with arms outstretched, and I went to hug her when she said, "No, no . . . let's pray." Early on, after the accident, I could not feel the power of other people's prayers, mostly because I was so numb and in shock. However, by this time, I could feel the power of the prayers that people were offering for us and so, naturally, I joyfully accepted. We held hands, and she began to praise Jesus. The more she praised Jesus, the more I praised Jesus. And then it happened.

I have never been able to describe what happened next accurately, mostly because I don't believe there are words in any language to describe what I experienced, but I'll try. With my eyes closed and while praising Our Lord, I felt what seemed like the softest, most plush blanket wrap around me. It had perfect depth and weight (much like our faith), and it squeezed me with what felt like the perfect hug, like that of a father hugging his son, and inside this "robe of righteousness" was warmth. Not just warmth, but energy and warmth. It was bliss and ecstasy and divine sublimity. It was love like no other. It was . . . heaven. And I felt God say, "This is only a taste of where Griffin is *all the time*." When we stopped praying, I had to look down at my feet because I was certain that I was floating!

That encounter was the beginning of a priority shift in my life. I now believed that Griffin was with his real Father. I now believed that Griffin was in a place that he would not, could not, ever want to leave, and I now believed that the plan for Griffin, for me, and for all of us was, in fact, divine. This encounter also allowed me to look back on my life and see my experiences with a new pair of glasses, spiritually mature glasses that enlightened my thinking and showed me things as God had seen them. For years, I lived and struggled with demons and situations that made me feel that life could never get any worse. I now began to realize that God, in his infinite wisdom and providence, was using those struggles to prepare me for something that far exceeded their pain. God was preparing me for Griffin's death and life without my son.

Shortly after Griffin's death, I was given the phone number of a man who had lost his son in a tragic accident some thirty years before. I put off calling him for a while, but then mustered the courage to talk to him. We talked for some time, and I asked him if there were days he wished more than anything that he could have his son back. Good Catholics who are strong in their faith and hold on to the sacraments can always be counted on to give great answers. He said, without hesitation, that if he had to go back to living the way he was when his son was alive, he would not want his son back. He went on to say that God had used his son's death to form him, to mold him, and to make him so much of a better man that he would have to be insane to want his former life. I couldn't believe him at the time, but after my experience with heaven, I started to see that nothing happens in God's world by mistake, including death and suffering. I began to see that suffering, especially redemptive suffering, is probably *the* most valuable tenet of our faith. I began to unite my suffering to Christ's suffering and see that he has always been with me and that he suffers with me . . . on the Cross.

My life today is still different, a little emptier and more lonesome and a little less meaningful without my son, but it also is more detached from worldly and secular beliefs, and fuller because of sincere relationships. I am more vulnerable and more transparent. More importantly, my life is more full of love. That greater love would not exist without the suffering in my life. One of the hardest things to accept for people who have never truly suffered is that suffering is an invitation to love. St. Louis Marie de Montfort wrote, "As wood is the fuel of flames, so the cross is the food of love." My heart has grown in love so much since Griffin's death. I have more empathy and am more compassionate than I ever was when he was with us. I have witnessed miracle after miracle of how omniscient our God is, and looking back on the days, weeks, and months after Griffin's death, I can see that those miracles were immediate. I watched a father and daughter reunite after years of division in the most beautiful embrace at Griffin's burial. I still get calls from fathers who tell me that there is not a night that goes by that they don't grab their sons and hug them and tell them how much they love them, when before, that kind of love was nonexistent.

The actions of many people have taught me much about our faith, and they may never even realize what they did for me. In his children is where I have found God more often than not these past four years. Since Griffin went home, I am more outspoken in my faith and more fervent in my love for Jesus. My veneration of Our Blessed Mother has become more intentional, my dependence on the prayers of saints more insistent, and my love of Jesus more evident. Today, it is personal. I was in Confession some time ago and confessed that I often think about wanting to see Griffin in heaven more than to stare into the eyes of Our Lord and sit at his banquet table. A holy priest asked me why I wanted to see Griffin (which seemed like a moronic question at the time). I said, "Because I love him." He then asked, "And what is God?" "God is Love," I replied. He told me to keep on wanting to see Griffin. So that is what I do. I live as though I want to see my son again. I laugh as much as I can, and I fix my eyes on heaven.

11

Losing a Young Adult Child

My Daughter's Death by Suicide

Deacon Ed Shoener

We know that all things work for good for those who
love God.

—Romans 8:28

I am told everyone reacts differently when the knock comes at your
door and you find out your child is dead. It was a knock that my wife,
Ruth, and I hoped would never come—but one that for more than
eleven years we had worried would come.

It was a few minutes before midnight on a warm Wednesday night
in August. The doorbell suddenly started ringing rapidly, and there was
loud knocking on our front door. I was upstairs in our bedroom with
Ruth, and we were just getting to sleep. I said to Ruth, "This can't be
good."

Ruth got to the door first and opened it. She said nothing, but she
looked at me startled. I got to the door to see two police officers and
immediately knew why they were there. Not a word was spoken until
I asked, "It's Katie, isn't it?"

The officers came in, and we walked silently to the kitchen, in shock but strangely composed. We all sat at the kitchen table, and I answered their questions. I was given the phone number of the officer in Ohio who found Katie and who was conducting the investigation. Katie lived near Columbus; we lived then and still do in Scranton, Pennsylvania. I called the officer immediately.

The officer in Ohio told me Katie died from a gunshot to her head. He had to ask difficult questions for the investigation. I assured him it was suicide—not a murder. I explained that Katie had lived with bipolar disorder for more than eleven years. She had attempted suicide before and struggled with intense suicidal thoughts. I asked him when we could bring her body home. The detective explained that the county coroner needed to conclude the investigation before we could do that.

I begged him to please finish the investigation quickly—that we wanted to bring our little girl home. It was at this point that I began to feel pain through the shock. It came slowly at first. Some tears as I talked to the officer. Ruth and I looked at each other, and we were just so, so sad. But we kept ourselves under control, showed the officers out, and thanked them for being so kind. We said we knew it was not easy for them to give parents this news. Then they quietly left our house.

More pain than I had ever felt hit me then, and hit hard. Ruth put her head down on the table. She weakened under the pain. She just cried and cried and cried inconsolably.

I had never known what it is to wail. It goes beyond tears. It is visceral. It is primordial. It comes from a place most of us never know exists within us. It is tears and screaming and physical pain. I went out on our deck and pounded our wooden table. I screamed and sobbed. Our son Bill built the table and made it strong and sturdy. I don't know how long I pounded on it. I pounded until I was exhausted.

At some point Ruth and I fell into each other's arms. Two became one. We needed each other. We were one stream of tears, like blood flowing from a wound. There is nothing sentimental about love at this moment. It is raw. It is horrible. Yet, in the face of death, it is life-giving.

It is strong, and it goes beyond all understanding. No words are spoken. Words are not possible or needed. Love is needed.

Katie's Mental Illness

Eventually Ruth and I started to talk. We did not know what else could have been done. Katie had done everything she was told to do by her doctors. She took all her medicines. She did not use drugs and was not addicted. Ruth talked to Katie every day—every single day. Katie's family loved her. She loved all of us, and she had many friends. She had recently graduated with her MBA from the Fisher College of Business at Ohio State University and wanted to work in human resource management because she loved helping people succeed.

We knew that Katie did not want to die by suicide. She wanted to live. She had attempted suicide before, and she was afraid of it. She had checked into a hospital several times when the suicidal thoughts were intense. She knew that suicide makes no sense. But mental illness is not rational. This illness told her that she was terrible, a burden, that no one liked or loved her, and that she was a useless mistake. She was in deep and irrational pain.

Mental illness is as evil and unrelenting as cancer, heart disease, or any other malady. For many people it can be treated and managed. Katie was treated by therapists and psychiatrists, and she took medicines for her type 1 bipolar disorder. Like chemotherapy for cancer, which can help people live longer than they would have without the chemotherapy, the medicines kept Katie alive for many years. But in her last year the medicines slowly stopped working. Her mental illness overwhelmed her and became lethal.

God's Grace and Katie's Obituary

Ruth and I finally went to bed the night our daughter died, but sleep was impossible. Full-on dad instincts kicked in for me. I felt a need to do what I could for my little girl. I got up and called the funeral director in the middle of the night. We talked about getting her home, about making funeral arrangements, about all the things you never want to do for your child. But at this moment you do them—and you want to do them well. Katie still needed to be taken care of.

I decided I needed to write Katie's obituary. Ruth asked me what I was doing at the computer. It was the middle of the night and only a couple of hours since the police knocked on our door. How, she wondered, could I possibly be able to write anything? But I wanted our friends, neighbors, and parishioners to know what happened so there would not be any gossip or hushed talk. I wanted them to know that Katie was a good girl who had a terrible illness. So, with the grace of God, I wrote Katie's obituary that night.

> Kathleen "Katie" Marie Shoener, 29, fought bipolar disorder since 2005, but she finally lost the battle to suicide on Wednesday in Lewis Center, Ohio.
>
> So often, people who have a mental illness are known as their illness. People say that "she is bipolar" or "he is schizophrenic." Over the coming days as you talk to people about this, please do not use that phrase. People who have cancer are not cancer, those with diabetes are not diabetes. Katie was not bipolar—she had an illness called bipolar disorder. Katie herself was a beautiful child of God. The way we talk about people and their illnesses affects the people themselves and how we treat the illness. In the case of mental illness, there is so much fear, ignorance, and hurtful attitudes that the people who suffer from mental illness needlessly suffer further.
>
> Our society does not provide the resources that are needed to adequately understand and treat mental illness. In Katie's case, she had the best medical care available, she always took the cocktail of medicines that she was prescribed, and she did her best to be healthy and manage this illness. And yet, that was not enough. Someday a cure will be found, but until then, we need to support and be compassionate to those with mental illness, every bit as much as we support those who suffer from cancer, heart disease, diabetes, or any other illness.

Please know that Katie was a sweet, wonderful person
who loved life, the people around her—and Jesus Christ.

Early that morning we made the calls you never want to make
to your children. We called Katie's three brothers—Rob, Bill, and
Eddie—to tell them their sister died by suicide. It was hard to hear
the anguish, deep sorrow, and weeping from them.

I sent out an email to my colleagues at my business with the obituary and asked for their patience while I took time for Katie's funeral. I
also sent an email with the obituary to the staff at St. Peter's Cathedral
in Scranton, where I am a permanent deacon. And then I went to the
8:00 a.m. Mass at the cathedral—the daily Mass I regularly attend.

Clinging to Christ, Broken for Us

I was drawn to the Eucharist that morning with the strongest pull I
had ever felt to attend a Mass. I entered the sacristy and saw Fr. Jeff
Walsh and others talking about the news of Katie's death. They were
surprised to see me. But where else would I go to find solace? I asked
to preach and explained to the small congregation why I needed to
be at the Mass that morning. I read Katie's obituary—slowly, so that
I would not sob and be incoherent—because it was important that
they heard the message clearly.

Like the love between Ruth and me when we had received the news
just a few hours earlier, there is nothing remote and sentimental about
the love that Christ offers at Mass. His love, then as always, was direct,
and I felt it. His Passion and Death were united to Katie's death and
to my grief during that Mass. He held me up. He was with me. Christ
went into my darkness, like walking into a tomb, to be with me. Katie
was broken, I was broken, and Christ's body was also broken for us at
the altar, as it is at every Mass. Christ was suffering with my family and
me. His presence in the Eucharist was never more real to me.

At the end of Mass, I went down the aisle to greet the small group
of people who attend the morning Mass. I needed to be surrounded by
this small Christian community that I worship with each day. Again,

it was not remote and sentimental; it was instead direct and real. All pretenses fell away.

In a community united in Christ, there is grief and sorrow, yet there is also strength and love; we lift one another up. Even if it was only a simple "I am so sorry," I could see in my community members' eyes the love of Christ as they said it. I knew once again Christ was broken for me by their compassion and loving presence.

I was scheduled to see my spiritual director, Fr. Jim Redington, for our monthly meeting that morning right after Mass. I kept the appointment. I walked the few blocks from the cathedral to the Jesuit residence at the University of Scranton, where my spiritual director lives. I told him about Katie. He knew how it felt to lose someone you love to suicide, telling me his brother died this way.

I am a spiritual director myself, and one of the fundamental beliefs about spiritual direction is that in every session there are three people: the directee, the director, and the Holy Spirit. Usually, the directee does most of the talking, the director asks questions and offers guidance, and both listen in their hearts for the Holy Spirit. At our session that morning, we went into the small chapel of Fr. Jim's residence and simply sat in adoration of the Eucharist. I could not talk, and he knew there was nothing he could say that would help right then. Only the Holy Spirit spoke that morning. We were enveloped in love.

I was given the gift of God's peace on the most horrible morning of my life: at Mass, with the support of my faith community, and while in eucharistic adoration with a holy priest who understood my pain. The peace of the Lord was with my spirit.

The Viral Obituary

The rest of that day was filled with calls and visits from family and friends, all deeply appreciated. That afternoon I went to meet with our funeral director to work out the details of the funeral. Ruth stayed at home to be with our family. I selected a white casket for Katie. White is the color of hope—hope in the resurrection.

Among the many other things that had to be done, we also put the details of the funeral into Katie's obituary and sent it to the local newspaper for publication in both the hard copy of the newspaper and the online version. It appeared the next day.

I had hoped the obituary would encourage an open and honest conversation about mental illness and Katie's suicide in our small town of Scranton, but what actually happened was totally unexpected. The response to Katie's obituary was incredible. It went viral in social media. It was picked up by newspapers throughout the United States and around the world. There was television and radio coverage. Katie's obituary was seen by millions of people, as headlines appeared in places near and far.

I am convinced, beyond any shadow of doubt, that God used Katie's obituary to deliver his message of love. God did not create Katie to have a mental illness and die by suicide; he created her to be the beautiful and vibrant person that we all knew and loved. Yet we live in a broken world where there is sin, illness, and death. All this evil will be completely defeated in eternal life, but evil is also overcome every day in this life, as God pours out his love on us in the small things of life, such as Katie's obituary, as a sign of what is to come in eternal life. God overcame Katie's tragic death by using her obituary to help people understand that he is with them in their struggle with mental illness and he has mercy on those who die by suicide.

Changed Forever

As consoling as all the notes and comments were, Ruth and I will, of course, always dearly miss Katie. Everyone whom I have spoken with who has buried a child has said there will always be a hole in our hearts. The shock has subsided, and we have gotten back to working and enjoying life, but we are forever changed.

The death of a child, especially by suicide, puts a tremendous strain and burden on a marriage. Depression, loneliness, and perhaps anger move in. All too often it leads to divorce. Ruth and I are fortunate that our marriage has endured, but it has changed. Grief is now a part of our marriage. Ruth and I grieve differently, but we can grieve together. We were bound together in a thousand ways, but now we are also bound together in Katie's death. In a mysterious way, the grace of the Holy Spirit that is part of the Sacrament of Matrimony has carried us in our grief.

At times our grief felt almost unbearable. Although its intensity has diminished with time, it has not gone away. We still think about Katie and her death every day. Everyone I have spoken to who has lost a child says the same. The grief that comes with losing a child is different from what comes with other losses. It is intense, and it is long lasting; perhaps it is forever. We need to pray for those who are living with the death of a child, and we need to pray for marriages that face this grief.

Finding Katie

From time to time I visit Katie's grave to grieve. There is a simple stone with a cross and her favorite saying engraved on it: "Be Awesome." But I know I will not find Katie at her grave. I know Katie is with the risen Christ.

As the angels said on the morning of the Resurrection, "Why do you seek the living one among the dead? He is not here, but he has been raised" (Lk 24:5–6). Christ is not dead but lives eternally. A fundamental truth of our faith is that Christ is in us and in everyone we encounter. Therefore, I will find Christ among the living, and where I find Christ is also where I will find Katie because Katie is with the risen Christ. Both are among the living.

We can find our loved ones in the things that they loved and in the things they struggled with, just as we can find Christ in our own loves and struggles. Katie loved to be around people, yet she struggled with mental illness and died by suicide. So, I find Katie not by grieving alone but by being around people and serving those who struggle with mental illness. In a special way, I see Christ in people who grieve a loved one who died by suicide.

Death is not the final word; even the tragedy of death by suicide is not the final word. The Word of God overcomes death and transforms it to new life. We can participate in this new life by seeing in the death of our loved ones an inspiration to build up the kingdom of God. We overcome the death of a loved one by taking what they loved and bringing that love to the world. We can take the suffering of our lives and transform it into loving service to others who suffer with what they suffered.

12

Losing an Adult Child

The Sacred Heart of Jesus

Lonny LaVerne

It was a normal February day. I had just dropped off my son, Christian, coming home from work around 5:25 p.m. Christian lived two doors down. I watched him walking toward his carport. He said, "I love you, Pop." And I replied, "I love you, son." About forty minutes later, I got a call saying something bad had happened to Christian. I ran over to his house. He was under the carport, lying face up. His legs were crossed and his eyes were wide open, dilated. He was not breathing. I knew this wasn't good. I tried to talk to him to comfort him, but there was no response.

All I remember is that I started praying. That's all I knew to do. I just started praying for him. I just kept praying and praying. I called a friend who came quickly. My friend asked me not to get mad at God. I said, "How can I get mad at God? Christian was God's before he belonged to us." In the meantime, a friend of Christian's, who was at his house to pick up some tools, began giving him CPR.

Next thing I knew, there were first responders at the house, and they took my son to the hospital. I prayed harder than ever. At the hospital, my wife and I discovered that Christian had an asymmetric brain aneurysm. The doctors wanted to fly him to another hospital, but every option kept getting shot down because of bad cloud cover. They ended up putting him in a critical-care ambulance to drive to Our Lady of the Lake Hospital in Baton Rouge.

I called our priest first thing. He's our go-to spiritual man. Father brought me back to the Church after living a hard life. Our priest is special, and he loved Christian. I also called a friend of ours who is an ER doctor at Our Lady of the Lake to tell him Christian was headed for their ER. My friend was at home and called back saying a team of doctors was waiting on Christian's ambulance.

After my wife and I arrived, we were reassured that everything that could be done was being done. We kept asking that they do more to help Christian, but multiple doctors told us he was in a coma and would not be getting better. We asked to see the brain scans. While scrolling through the scans with the assistant, we saw an image of the Sacred Heart of Jesus in the scans. Seeing this brought acceptance and peace. When we saw the heart, we thought that was Christian saying, "Goodbye, I love you."

In addition to asking for more to be done, we requested the presence of a priest to administer the Sacrament of the Anointing of the Sick. We were able to get that. During that time, we had decisions to make. We had a discussion about Christian being an organ donor. We knew Christian would want that. Someone from the Louisiana Organ Procurement Agency (LOPA) came quickly, sat with us, and explained everything. When we made that decision the wheels started turning, and he had to be prepared for the donation surgery.

After the paperwork was signed, we went outside and LOPA raised the hero's flag under the American flag. Police and hospital representatives were there at the flag raising. There was no wind. But once they raised the flag, the wind started blowing, and the flag started waving. And they said once everything was complete with Christian, they would send us the flag. We still have it.

Christian was thirty-seven years old. He died from a brain aneurysm. Our priest, even though he was leaving the country, found a way to do Christian's Funeral Mass. At the Mass and burial, the enormous number of people who showed up for Christian was striking. The crowds just kept coming. Also, about sixteen men, friends of the family, came to pray the Rosary. Nobody left at the departing of the family. Everyone stayed to pray.

I wanted to read the readings at Christian's funeral. The priest wasn't sure I could make it through that, but I knew I could, and it's what Christian would want. My wife had back issues before the funeral and couldn't stand on a hard surface for more than thirty to forty-five minutes. Well, she stood for four hours, not wanting to leave the casket and wanting to greet everyone in line. Her back did not hurt one time, and she has had no back issues since.

God's hand is in Christian's story. God is in every story. Christian loved his name. He didn't want to be called Chris. His name was who he was. Christian helped a lot of people doing work on the side. He was really good at plumbing and the like. He would help anyone who couldn't afford to pay him. One older lady with a handicapped son needed her bathroom redone. Christian didn't believe in boasting because, as he would say, "You gotta get your blessings" and "God don't like ugly." He asked the lady to save up for the materials, but she didn't need to pay anything for labor. Christian had a friend help him, the same guy who called 911 and started CPR on Christian until the EMTs arrived. Christian was going to give this guy some tools for helping with the bathroom, which is why the friend was at Christian's when he collapsed. If Christian hadn't helped this elderly lady and recruited his friend, then he wouldn't have been found and received CPR, and he would not have received the last rites, and we wouldn't have seen his brain scans. The blessings that Christian extended to others came back to us.

I had the Sacred Heart of Jesus enthroned at my house and hung the image. Every time Christian's daughter left my house, she would kiss Jesus's heart. All of this gave our family great comfort. Plus, our priest told us, "Your son is in heaven," and to pray to him. I don't know if Father is right or wrong, but those words sure sounded good to me.

I lost Christian in February, lost my brother at the end of March, I was diagnosed with cancer at the end of April, had surgery for my cancer in June, and had chemo for the rest of that year. The whole time we kept getting signs from Christian. At the hospital, we went to the chapel to give thanks. Everywhere we went, people were touched by our story about Christian. It was as if God was leading us to encounter people who needed to hear it. People even asked if they could share our story with others. Of course we didn't mind, because it's important for people to know there is something beyond this life.

I was used to being with Christian all the time. He worked by my side his whole life. After he died, I didn't want to go back to work. I had lost my son, coworker, best friend, hunting buddy, fishing buddy, confidant. I just didn't know what I was going to do. My world was obliterated. I didn't have any answers.

My wife and I decided we would go wherever God wanted us to go. We didn't know what else to do. We fell completely into God's loving arms and care. Eventually, God's answers kept coming. Red Bird Ministries was one of those answers. All along the journey, God kept showing up in the people we met, places we would go, and especially our fellow parishioners. The greatest gifts were the people God placed in our lives. He seemed to send us whatever we needed. Fortunately, God gave us the faith to humbly accept the tragedy of Christian's death. I don't know what we would have done without our faith. Our hearts were torn open, and then God filled them full.

I can still be triggered to grieve. My grief can be triggered by anything—a fleeting memory, a smell, something somebody says at work. Christian had a lot of clichés that belonged only to him and had an accent that cannot be replicated. His wife called Christian her knight in shining camouflage. He loved to cook, and he cooked the best crawfish; no one could beat it. He loved to dance, and he loved good old-fashioned country music. I'm so thankful for all the pictures we have of him.

Christian had his own spiritual life. He was a man of prayer. We prayed together, and he openly expressed his feelings. He always told me he loved me. He wasn't even embarrassed to kiss his dad in public. In my spiritual life, I learned a lot from my son. God has showed himself to me in Christian's life. God made his presence known to me through Christian.

I'm very proud to have had him as my son, because of the man he was. I'm talking about the person that he was, the whole being. What you saw was what you got. He didn't pretend to be someone he was not. I reflect back on his life, his death, and our relationship and see that God had a very strong hand in all of it.

God's presence has come full circle through Christian's daughter—her love for God the Father, Jesus, and Mary. She loves Mass and says everybody ought to go. At four years old, after Christian's death, she even said she saw her daddy at Mass.

Losing a child is hard, and to a father who has just lost a child, I would say to be grateful for all that God has given you. Try not to cut yourself short on what you could have done or what you didn't do, and concentrate on the most important thing, which is what you had and what you have. Memories of life are priceless. Moments in that life shared together can't be measured. Always try to be humble and thank God for everything. Even in the bad, if we look hard enough, there is good to be found. Don't ask, "Why?" or "Why me?" Ask, "Why not me?" If God wants me to know why, he'll tell me. Answers will come when you're not even asking questions. We have to be silent to listen for the Lord.

13

Losing an Adult Child

No Greater Love

Richard Phillis, MD

Ever since our son, Stephen, was six years old, he dreamed of flying in the military. This desire was planted in his heart after visiting the Air Force Academy. From that moment, Stephen was set on flying in the US Air Force. After all, fighter pilots are often first-born children like Stephen. Naturally, the oldest child tends to have the strongest will. You could say he was destined or called by God.

In high school, Stephen took his studies seriously and loved playing defensive back on the football team. Following high school, he set off for the Air Force Academy and graduated in 1982. My now-late wife, Diane, and I fully supported him. We knew the risks involved when Stephen entered the armed forces, but we were not going to hold him back. He would spend nine years as a pilot doing what he loved.

Eventually, Stephen became an air force captain. With the start of the Gulf War in January 1991, we knew that his life could be in even more danger, especially because he would be flying on serious missions in a very risky aircraft. He suggested to us the possibility that he might not survive—yes, the conflict was real. We always had this in the back of our minds, but we realized he was doing what he wanted to do.

Then one day we heard a knock at our door, a knock every parent of a child in the military dreads. It was two air force officers notifying us that our son's A-10 fighter plane had been shot down over northwestern Kuwait on February 15, 1991. Despite not knowing if our son was still alive, we had reason to hope. We continually thought he would be found. And so, we prayed daily for his safety. We heard of other prisoners of war who had been released, so perhaps he was being held hostage by the Iraqis. Each day, the colonel from Stephen's division would call us with updates. Many people, including members of Stephen's high school community, Alleman in Rock Island, Illinois, offered prayers for him. A special Mass was even offered.

When my wife was interviewed during the time of Stephen's disappearance, she said, "[Stephen] believed in what he was doing, and he loved what he was doing, so I have no regrets. I think this is a great country, and our five children have always felt it worth defending with their lives."[1] At the time, my wife and I were fifty-five years old, and Stephen was thirty.

A few weeks later we received a phone call from the air force saying they had found remains. They asked us to submit a blood sample for DNA. During the wait, we kept praying that Stephen might still be alive—that is, until our DNA matched with the identified remains. Because of how dangerous our son's mission was, the outcome did not surprise us. Still, no parent wants to receive the news that their child has died.

At his Funeral Mass on April 18 at St. Pius X Catholic Church, more than two months after his death, we learned that Stephen had been awarded the Silver Star.[2] According to Stephen's wingman and first lieutenant Robert Sweet, my son had sacrificed his life to protect Robert, who was shot down by ground fire.[3] Stephen's heroic actions were not new to us. He was a giving person—he always thought of others, seldom of himself.

My wife and I didn't hesitate to talk about Stephen to our other children, who were also grieving the loss of their brother. We were not the only ones who mourned Stephen's passing. In fact, the night before going to the Persian Gulf, he had proposed to his fiancée, who still keeps in touch with us.

At the time Stephen died, there was another military family in our area who lost a son in the Gulf War. We reached out to the parents to see if we could help. But they were not interested in anything we had to say. As a result, we decided not to reach out to other military parents who lost a child, especially if we did not know them. My wife and I realized that all of these people have their families and support system. Sometimes people don't want others to intrude. However, when there is a report of some military member dying, we empathize with the families in our minds and offer our prayers.

God's grace has enabled me to face Stephen's death and absence with peace. I've always had a good relationship with God, and I still do. And I realize that sometimes things I ask him for I am not going to get. Sometimes he says no. But by and large, God has been with me when I needed him. And he has always helped me when I have had major decisions to make and has guided me in making the right choice.

I am a great believer that water flows under the bridge and never flows back. I try not to relive the past, wondering if such-and-such event could have been prevented; instead, I look to the future. God has his plan. We don't always know what it is. Hence, when Stephen died, I didn't question his will, but I prayed. I tried not to linger in my grief. I believe that a person ought to do what the circumstances and information seem to indicate is best. But a man can't live with regrets—you leave things in God's hands. God does what is best. We can't change some things, so I do the best I can to embrace God's will.

Through the years, I have realized that grief is something you can't describe until you experience it. And everybody grieves in a different way. It's an ongoing process. When we lost Stephen, we were amazed at the number of people who showed concern, especially our parish family. To this day, I occasionally meet someone who refers to Stephen. In fact, others still honor his memory, especially on the anniversary of his death. We realize that other people are sharing Stephen's death with us on a regular basis. And that he is not forgotten. This has really helped my grieving process.

Although my wife and I did not reach out to other military couples who lost a child because of the first experience we had, it's important to attend the wake and funeral of people you know . . . to let them know that you are also sharing to some degree in their pain.

When people ask me about my children, I say that God blessed us with Stephen along with his four siblings. We raised our children to live virtuous lives. And we showed them by example. We never pressured them to follow a certain career. When our son said he was going to enter the military, we supported him. In fact, three of our five children served in the military. And the other two couldn't enter for various reasons.

My late wife and I knew that providing a nurturing and loving home between husband and wife was the key to giving our children the security they needed to thrive in life. Our Catholic faith, especially Mass and prayer, sustained us through the years.

Although it has been more than thirty years since my son passed away, I still think of him every day—because when you lose a child, you never forget. The day of my son's passing is always fresh in my mind, along with Stephen's Funeral Mass. I remember what a great homily Fr. Daniel Mirabelli delivered. He reiterated Stephen's bravery. And the kiss of peace was particularly emotional for the family. I still make a note of February 15—Stephen's passing. I don't do anything specific to remember him. But I still visit his grave from time to time.

The thought of being reunited with my son and now my late wife in heaven has helped me to move forward. Our goal in life is to lay down our lives for others as Christ did. There is no greater love than Christ's love on the Cross, which my son strove to imitate by laying down his life for God and country, including his fellow wingman.

Part III
PRACTICAL WISDOM, REFLECTIONS, PRAYERS, and SCRIPTURE PASSAGES

14

The Mystery of Suffering

Joseph Pearce

The mystery of suffering, or what C. S. Lewis called the problem of pain, is at the very heart of the human experience. It has animated and confounded the philosophers and has inspired some of the greatest literature. The book of Job grapples with it. Homer and Sophocles struggle with it. Yet the Hebrew prophets and the Greek pagans were at a disadvantage. They knew nothing of the Cross, nor of the Son of God who was sacrificed on it. It is in the darkness of Golgotha that light shines on the mystery of suffering. It is the Cross that provides the priceless clue to the solving of the problem of pain. It is when we see the innocence of the Victim hanging from the Cross that we begin to see that we never suffer alone, even in the very darkest of times, *especially* in the very darkest of times.

This consoling truth is revealed on Golgotha by the crucified Christ, but also by the two criminals being crucified on either side of him. The good thief confesses his sin and accepts the just punishment for it, asking for forgiveness and receiving it. The bad thief refuses to confess any culpability for his actions, cursing his suffering and demanding of God to be freed from it. The first thief accepts his suffering with humility and is rewarded with the gift of heaven, becoming a saint in paradise. The other thief curses his suffering with pride and condemns himself to hell. They have been given the same penalty for their sins, but they respond very differently. Suffering is a gift, and it's all about how we accept it.

This understanding of the mystery of suffering was encapsulated with succinct brilliance by Oscar Wilde in *The Ballad of Reading Gaol*, the poem inspired by his experience of a two-year prison sentence. "God's eternal Laws are kind and break the heart of stone," he wrote, for "how else but through a broken heart may Lord Christ enter in." Oscar Wilde was a great sinner and for many years was unrepentant, yet, like the good thief in the gospel, he was received by Christ into the Church on his deathbed. It is in this way that a great sinner can become a saint, through the acceptance of the suffering that is given, knowing that it is a priceless gift with the power to break the prideful heart, making room for Christ to enter in and heal it.

I know this from bitter experience. I know it from the bottom of my own broken heart. I know it from the depths of the darkness of desolation. I know it from my own very personal "very darkest of times." I know it from the moment that I held in my arms the cold, lifeless body of my stillborn baby daughter.

My wife, Susannah, and I were expecting our second child. All was well until the horrible day when Susannah noticed that the baby, now nearly eight months old in utero, seemed to have stopped kicking or even moving. Our worst fears became a real and living nightmare when a scan revealed that there was no heartbeat. Our dear little child had died before seeing the light of day, only four weeks before her due date.

My poor wife! Whatever I might have been feeling, I could not imagine what she was going through. Labor was induced and Susannah had to go through all the pains of childbirth, aware that she would be giving birth to a stillborn baby. We had not wished to know the baby's sex ahead of time, and I remember so clearly the moment that our lifeless child was placed in Susannah's arms. "It's a girl!" she exclaimed, her eyes filling with tears of both grief and joy.

A short while later, I found myself sitting cross-legged on the bed, cradling our daughter, whom we named Gianna, in my arms. I looked up at the crucifix on the wall and found myself, for the first and only time in my life, being lifted up onto the Cross. I felt myself at one with my crucified Lord. He was embracing me, making my suffering his own. But, more than that, I felt myself being crucified with him. He and I were one. I had never felt myself as close to Christ, fully united with him on the Cross, and I have never since felt myself as close to him. What a bittersweet blessing!

Every other time that I have found myself gazing at a crucifix in prayer, both before and since that fateful day, I see myself nailing my Lord to the Cross. It is my sins that have nailed him there. It is my sins that crown him with thorns. It is my sins that pierce his side. This is as it should be. I am a miserable sinner, and my Lord suffers the agonies of his Passion for my sins. But once and once only, on a sorrowful and glorious day, my Lord and Savior lifted me up onto the Cross with him, embracing me, uniting himself with me.

But what of that other innocent victim? What of our little girl? Will she not share the life of the Innocent Victim himself, being raised with Christ to everlasting life? Please, Lord, let it be so. Praised be Jesus Christ!

15

Letter from Our Eucharistic Lord to a Grieving Father

I am with you always, until the end of the age.
—Matthew 28:20

Beloved, I know your pain and suffering more than anyone, just as my Father knows every hair on your head. I know your anger. I know your sadness. I know your loneliness. I know your anxiety. I know your disappointment. Yes, I see your grief and sorrow because I have borne my own terrible Cross. You do not have to hide your sorrows from me, nor let them weigh you down. My Eucharistic Heart present in this tabernacle is not scandalized by your misery, nor does it delight in your suffering. My Eucharistic Heart only seeks to love you and hide you in my wounds.

I am not oblivious to this greatest of sorrows, the loss of your beloved child, whom I have known from the beginning. I also love your child and remember the day your child was conceived. All of heaven rejoiced. I remember the day your child was born. I know you can recall that day, too, for it was one of the happiest days of your life. And I remember the day your child died. All of heaven mourned. I know you can recall that day like it was yesterday, for it was one of the worst days of your life. I understand your grief more than anyone, even you. I, too, grieved—when I lost my father Joseph, my cousin John the Baptist, my friend Lazarus. I, too, wept.

Sometimes you wonder why your child died while others have never known such a loss. In heaven, I will tell you why your child's life ended so abruptly. But for now, I want you to know this: when your child died, you and your child were with me on the Cross. Although you might have felt forsaken, it was in that moment that I was the closest to you. It was in that moment that I stretched out my pierced hand and drew you to my pierced heart. I was carrying you then.

Perhaps you are still angry with me for not saving your child. But do not flee from me, because I only want to help you. No earthly pleasures will dull the pain of losing your child, because only my Eucharistic Heart can heal you and give you true peace. Someday you will see that I always bring good out of evil. Good triumphs in the end, because love is stronger than death.

Remember, beloved, that all things come to an end, including your present grief and suffering. This passing world is not your home. You were made for heaven, not earth. Never forget how much I love you and what awaits you in heaven. For if you truly knew what is on the other side, you would long for it with all of your heart. Soon your tears will be turned into joy.

I know you cannot wait to see and hold your child again. But know this—your child is with me, enclosed in my Eucharistic Heart. For I am the God of the living, the God of the past, the present, and the future. So be at peace. My mother, Mary, is also with me, for wherever I am, so is she. When you visit me, never forget her sorrows. My mother also longs to heal your broken heart, for she knows your pain more than any person on earth. She knows what it is like to bury both her Lord and her son. Call upon my mother, and she will lead you on the path of healing, for she is the Comfort of the Afflicted.

Although at times you do not feel my presence, I am always here waiting for you in the Most Blessed Sacrament. Day and night, I am a prisoner of love, eagerly waiting to console you. Yes, "I am with you always, until the end of the age" (Mt 28:20). So come to me, and lay your grieving heart on my Eucharistic Heart, and I will give you rest. I will give you the strength you need to carry this cross, for you do not carry it by yourself. Behold, I suffer with you. And one day, I, too, will take you to my Father's house, where you shall never again be separated from me and your child.

16

Letter from a Clinician to a Grieving Father

Johnathan M. Sumpter, MBA, MA, LPC-S, NCC
Director, University of Dallas Counseling Center
Founder and CEO, The Mental Well, PLLC

Brothers of loss, intimate partners who share the loss, fellow clinicians, ministers, and other supporters of men who have lost a child, I want to take a moment to honor and lift each of you and the ones who were lost. I pray this book has been or will be as consoling for you as it was for me.

As a clinician, I am often drawn to Luke 4:23. In this passage, Jesus anticipates a defensive rebuke from the Pharisees with the words, "Physician, cure yourself." This rebuke was a provocation for proof of what he preached. Jesus responded by informing them that this alone did not prove or disprove the truth of his message. I, however, am not Jesus. I am not the Divine Physician. As a clinician, I do not possess any ability to heal myself. In the throes of grief, proof of Jesus's message, that of Divine Love, was known in my head but not readily accessible in my heart.

I spent more than a decade in ministry, several years as a certified spiritual director, and some years as a diocesan seminarian. I have spent more than a decade as a licensed psychotherapist in many clinical settings (including an NICU) and several years supervising others learning to become clinicians. I have held various other positions in supportive settings. I have helped countless individuals carry their crosses through pain, suffering, struggle, and grief.

Despite my experience, I am not exempt from the crushing weight of profound personal grief. Two of our living children were nearly lost at ages two weeks and four years old to different illnesses. We lost four of our children before birth—Samuel, Therese, Christopher, and Caleb Roch Sumpter. I have lost loved ones and experienced various forms of grief. However, the loss of each of my children was grief on a whole different level.

A first responder cannot perform CPR if he is the one having a heart attack. A lifeguard cannot give herself mouth-to-mouth resuscitation. A clinician cannot help heal grief if it is his own. This message is valid for every human. Grief can shake us regardless of what we have known. No one can be the savior to their own mortal humanity.

Grief is the most profound experience of the human condition—a devastating state of contradictions of the extremes of humanity all felt at once. Until a person moves through grief long enough to not be utterly crushed by it, he will not fully understand it. Thus, the experience of grief is not easy to articulate.

Because grief is difficult to articulate, meeting one's needs can be tantamount to solving an astrophysics equation without grasping introductory calculus. That is why grief needs to be met with compassion, mercy, dignity, and grace. Grief is not something to be fixed, prayed away, or even entirely removed. Grief is experienced in the moment, honored, and continually moved through. Grief becomes less acutely crushing but no less meaningful over time as it is moved through. Grief is something that eventually leads to a deeper meaning—maybe much later. Even with my experience and training, I had no understanding of profound grief until the loss of a child.

Those who support men of loss would do well to offer them encouragement by being present, praying, and keeping time and energy available for them. Do not try to talk them out of grief. Show them you stand side by side with them as they move through it. Help them be present with what they are going through. May this book be a starting point to help the grieving man of faith and those who care for him face and move through the human condition to God's ultimate message of healing and love.

17

Advice for a Grieving Father

Pray: Praying after a child loss can be challenging; it's hard to know what to say. In those times, resting in the quietness of the Holy Spirit can be enough. The Holy Spirit can lead our prayer: "In the same way, the Spirit too comes to the aid of our weakness; for we do not know how to pray as we ought, but the Spirit itself intercedes with inexpressible groanings" (Rom 8:26).

Even if you feel nothing, pray. The greater the struggle, the greater the grace God wants to pour into your soul. When you are wounded, the enemy seeks to destroy you. He whispers in your ear: "Where is your loving God now? Your wife doesn't care about you. No one understands your pain." During this greatest of trials, Jesus wants to draw you closer to his sacred wounds. Our Lady, Mother of Sorrows, wants to comfort your afflictions by wrapping you in her mantle. She invites you to pray the Rosary and to visit her Eucharistic son, who knows exactly what you are going through. Yes, Our Lord and Our Lady understand your pain more than anyone. Our Lady knows what it is like to lose her only son and her God. She wants to accompany you as she accompanied her son to Calvary. Above all, her son, the Good Shepherd, longs to carry you in his arms through this valley of darkness.

Acknowledge Your Emotions: It's perfectly normal to feel anger, depression, and isolation. You are not a bad Christian if you are upset with God. In fact, the opposite is true. The closest friends share the most intimate details, the good and the bad. The closest friends understand each other's hearts. Our Lord once told a twentieth-century mystic, Gabrielle Bossis, "I know all about your emotions as I know every wave of the sea. Even before you speak I hear you, since I live in you."[1] Our emotions are not sinful in themselves; they simply arise from our interaction with life situations. Many times, especially when the situation is extreme, we feel the urge to respond to or act on our emotions. But we cannot let emotions lead us into sinful actions or dictate how we live. Don't let your emotions carry you away to dark places. Instead, ask God for guidance and channel your emotions to pursue virtue.

Address Your Anger: Of all the emotions that arise after child loss, anger toward God is the most natural and common among men. Like King David and so many saints, we must cry out to God rather than retreat from him. There are many ways to address anger in a healthy, nonharmful way. The first is by being totally transparent with God. Yes, he sees your pain, but he also longs to hear about it. He longs for you to cry out to him with tears, to rip your chest open to him, because he ripped open his Sacred Heart on the Cross for you. Perhaps you will even get on your knees and grab a crucifix and pray with Christ: "My God, my God, why have you forsaken me?" (Mt 27:46). When your anger toward God makes you give up on him or stop praying to him, then it is time to seek him in the Sacrament of Penance by going to Confession.

On a natural level, unhealthy anger toward God, if left unchecked, can easily be taken out on others. When the moments of anger surge in your heart, it may be time to do something physical. Go for a run. Lift weights. Put on some uplifting music. Do something fun with your spouse. It is important to pay attention to what triggers the anger. Journal your thoughts. Perhaps even write a letter to Jesus in the Holy Eucharist, telling him all that frustrates you.

Trust: God is in control. There are some great spiritual books that can guide you, particularly on the topic of trust, such as *Arise from Darkness*, by Fr. Benedict Groeschel; *Trustful Surrender to Divine Providence*, by Fr. Jean Baptiste Saint-Jure and St. Claude de la Colombière; and *Abandonment to Divine Providence*, by Fr. Jean-Pierre de Caussade. Trust is the path to true peace.

Seek Out a Counselor or Spiritual Director: The idea of seeing and talking to a counselor may seem like you are giving up your ability to deal with grief by yourself or in your own way. But opening up to a third party, someone who can be objective about your situation, can provide much-needed clarity about your feelings. Importantly, a clinical specialist can determine if your grief has developed into clinical depression, anxiety, or post-traumatic stress disorder. If so, your grief may need more focused and directed attention or therapy.

One way a counselor can determine whether your grief needs more focused therapy is through specially designed questions. Sometimes these questions are asked as part of your routine doctor visits since our mental health is just as important as our physical health. A few of these questionnaires appear in part IV of this book. You might find it useful to use one of these tools to initiate conversations with a counselor.

If you do seek guidance from a counselor, we recommend finding a practicing Catholic since they should have a clear understanding of your human dignity and an awareness and respect for the root of your grief. Speaking with a spiritual director—a priest or religious, if possible—will provide an explicitly spiritual perspective of your loss and journey of grief. Understanding our sufferings in the context of faith can help provide clarity, hope, and a direction toward healing. Accepting our sufferings in the light of God's love and providence can go a long way in providing peace and healing.

Connect: Find other grieving fathers in your parish, diocese, or workplace to meet with for coffee, or invite them and their families to your house for dinner. You share something others may never understand. You are fathers of loss and brothers of the Cross.

Appreciate: Even though your world is falling apart, strive to find one thing each day for which to be grateful. It might be the morning sunrise or an evening sunset. It could be your wife's cooking or a random act of kindness someone sent your way. Each night before you go to bed, thank God for his goodness present throughout your day and give thanks for three particular things. Never forget your blessings.

Deepen Your Relationships: Go deeper in your relationships with your spouse and your living children if you are blessed to have them. "Put out into deep water," as Our Lord told St. Peter (Lk 5:4). Spend more time with them. Try to give them your undivided attention—actual face time. You will never regret spending too much time with your family, but you will regret spending too little time with them. They need your affection and support now more than ever. They too are suffering.

Rely on the Holy Spirit: Be open to the Holy Spirit, who dwells in every soul that is in a state of grace. The Holy Spirit is the true navigator of your soul. Perhaps there is some lesson he wants to teach you or someone he will inspire you to help in their grief as well. Most of all, the Holy Spirit wants to conform you more closely to Christ. Allow him to use your grief and suffering for the greater glory of God the Father.

Let Christ Define You: As great as children are, they cannot be the source of our identity as men. Our relationship with Christ must be what defines us. When we stand before God at our judgment, he will not ask us how many children we had. He will ask if we love him and if we led the children he gave us, no matter how long they lived, to his Sacred Heart.

18

Advice for Grieving Wives/Loss Moms

Kelly Breaux

Oh, grieving mother! My heart has found you here, in the middle of the storm that rages in your heart. Death has become too familiar to your family, and it is awful to know its sting. You may feel as if you are all alone, desperately trying to keep your family together. You may feel that your life is slipping through your fingers like sand as time ticks by and you feel increasingly isolated in the cavern of your darkness. You are not alone, sweet mama. Child loss is as awful as it sounds. As I sit thinking of each of you who will read this chapter, I cannot help but feel so much love for you. I know the blueprint of your grieving heart, how it longs to retrace the time and revisit the spaces when your child was with you—either inside your womb full of life or with you in your arms, making memories and chasing dreams.

Time now seems to move in slow motion. Some days you think it stands still. Maybe the loss was long ago but feels like only yesterday. You long to be in that moment once again, blinded by the pain and reality of your loss. Maybe you are feeling alone and misunderstood. That is so common, but know that you are loved and supported in prayer. This chapter was written just for you as a grieving mother and loving wife to a grieving father. As you process your own pain, your husband, your child's father, is with you in the middle of the darkness. When the grief overshadows us, sometimes we forget that someone else cares how much we are hurting. I know you can feel desperate and overwhelmed as you search to find the keys to healing. I hope this chapter will help you to understand the heart of your husband through my experience as another grieving mother and wife. I pray this chapter will unlock some of the mystery behind how you and your husband are likely grieving so differently from each other.

There are so many things that I want to say to you, but I must first echo the words of the Father's heart for you. There comes a point in our grief journey when words of truth are gems we uncover, rediscover, and treasure. We all need to be reminded from time to time of the promises of our faith and the love that God holds for each one of us. When truth becomes distorted, and the fog of grief wishes to claim our thinking and our identity, we can find ourselves in a crisis of faith and fall into believing lies about our spouses and ourselves.

During Mass one Sunday in Advent in 2022, I prayed intentionally about writing this chapter. "Lord, what will I tell them? You have the words of eternal life. Speak to me what you want them to know." God is so faithful and spoke these words into my heart to bring comfort and hope to yours: "Love can be restored. Your husband is not your savior; I am. Let *me* love all of you—the broken pieces, the forgotten pieces, the parts of you that you are ashamed of. I want to redeem your broken heart and restore love back to the right order, but you have to surrender your plan, your will to mine. Will you let me love you?"

In 2005, my husband and I found out that we were expecting twins. I was in a season of satisfaction with my life. I had been married to my best friend for three years, and we had the ooey-gooey kind of young love that some people poke fun at. The thing that most attracted me to Ryan was how I felt about myself when I was with him. I could be authentic and vulnerable with him. In addition to being charming, handsome, and a jokester, he was an incredible partner in life. The days were filled with laughter and adventure. He wanted me to go everywhere with him, and I did. During the early years of our marriage, life was simple, but suffering soon came knocking and rocked us both to the core.

When we learned there were two babies in my womb—a boy and a girl—we fell instantly in love with them and life seemed pretty perfect. How did things unravel so quickly? How did we go from wonderful to catastrophic so fast?

My pregnancy was uneventful until my twenty-eighth week. I woke to severe labor pains. Ryan and I rushed to the hospital just in time for the medical team to stop labor with the understanding that I would remain in their care until the twins were born. Sadly, my placenta abrupted a few hours later and the twins were delivered via emergency cesarian section. On October 16, 2005, at 1:28 p.m., Talon and Emma Grace were born. Both babies were extremely small and immediately needed medical attention. The prematurity of the babies left them susceptible to deadly infections and viruses. Talon died fifteen days later from pseudomonas sepsis with Emma Grace joining him in heaven just a little shy of four years later.

With the twins both gone, I found myself at the bottom of a black hole that I did not know how to climb out of. Nothing made sense anymore. Everything I thought I knew about how to survive awful situations failed me. I felt so alone in the middle of that darkness, desperate for someone to come and pull me out of the nightmare. Where was my knight in shining armor? Why wasn't he ready to save his princess from the dark tower as the dragon tried to devour her? But no one came, not even my husband. When I most needed the man that I loved and adored, I felt abandoned. He had no idea how to help me through my darkness because he was right there in the middle of it too. I failed to recognize his pain and could only see all the ways he failed me. I expected him to fix my pain. I wanted him to be my savior. There were days I snapped in my anger at him because he just couldn't figure out how much I thought I needed him.

This was such a tall order for a man who was also devastated and felt helpless in his inability to put our broken family back together.

Ryan was grieving too, but I failed to acknowledge his pain because he couldn't share his emotions with me verbally. As a young boy, he was taught that men do not cry, so as he grew into a man, he thought this was how a man handled crisis. He thought he had to be stoic, and his heart became hard, even to me. We were living through the same crisis but processed it so very differently from the other. We never really talked about our struggles. Internally, I hung on to my pain, and Ryan clung to his. We coped by stuffing our grief and attempting to avoid the elephant in the room.

We were broken, spiritually and emotionally disconnected. We didn't pray together. I never saw him cry in front of me, even in the privacy of our home. I honestly believed that Ryan did not love our children the way I did. Slowly that lie affected how I received his love for me. I never saw him wrestle with the emotional turmoil of the twins' death. I later learned that he hid his pain from me in an attempt to protect me from more suffering, but at the time I was left feeling emotionally abandoned. I began to think that there was something seriously wrong with me. How was I the only one losing it, falling apart on the bathroom floor? But instead of vulnerably sharing my needs and twisted thoughts and feelings with him, I stuffed them deep inside of me. Stuff, stuff, stuff, until the pot came to a full boil and I bubbled over with rage. Instead of turning the heat down on my inner turmoil by talking with Ryan, I felt intense anger. It always simmered slightly below the surface. My unspoken anger and resentment further hurt our family. My broken heart wanted nothing more than for others to hurt as much as I did, even Ryan.

As I journeyed through my own grief, I began to see that everyone responds to loss differently and that there are generally discernible differences in how men and women grieve. A light bulb went on for me as I uncovered this pearl of wisdom. I wish I would have known this early in my grief, before it nearly destroyed our marriage. Men often retreat to the workshop as St. Joseph might have. Women ponder things in their hearts like the Bible tells us Mary did. This was a foreign concept to me. But what did it actually mean?

Many men like to grieve in action by fixing things, tearing things down, or breaking things apart. This may seem aggressive, but it is a helpful way for them to process their emotions. While women tend to process their grief verbally or emotionally, many men are logical processors and may come to accept their loss more easily than women. Men usually use fewer words than women to articulate what they are trying to say and use speech that contains facts and data to solve problems. Men often leave out personal or anecdotal information. They may also try to dominate a conversation and can interrupt without realizing they have done so. Conversations from the male perspective are often more pragmatic, and conveying information becomes the primary purpose or goal. When a woman shares her feelings, men tend to want to identify and solve the problem, only to find that in grief, you can't fix your wife. This can further frustrate a husband.

Many women use a "rapport" style of communication that aims to express an idea, increase social connection, and build relationship. Women want to feel supported, heard, understood, and loved. Women often wish to discuss a problem in order to process how they are feeling, not necessarily to solve the problem. When a woman's spouse offers a solution, she does not feel heard and may lament that he does not understand or care about her feelings. She just wants her feelings to be acknowledged and heard.

Many women, perhaps even most, benefit from verbally processing their emotions with another person. A woman will often share very personally and draw the other person into her experience. Women tend to be more empathetic than men and hold space for others. When one family member is hurting, a woman holds their grief too.

Surprisingly, the majority of problems (or arguments) that couples of loss experience do not demand problem solving. Grief support typically only requires the presence of the other and their attuned, compassionate listening. When it's time to talk about important issues, try to share all relevant facts and feelings so you can intimately connect and talk things through as a team. Your husband is not your enemy. He is your best friend. It's important for you both to have an opportunity to express yourself and feel acknowledged, heard, and validated. Together you can respect each other's feelings and struggles and see each other clearly in the wasteland of your grief.

In order to communicate more effectively in grief, men and women need to process their feelings together as they learn to empathize and hear the other's subjective experience. The way we grieve the loss of our child and communicate that with words is going to be different. What stirs in our hearts is also going to be different, but we can still accept each other's grief, yoke ourselves to our spouse, and together carry the cross of child loss. You can't arrive ahead of your spouse. He is depending on you to be on this journey with him. And ditto for the dads.

This may feel like a lot to think about. It takes time to acclimate yourself to this type of communication with your spouse. I won't say it's easy, but I promise it will be worth it. Your marriage will change for the better by learning to communicate openly and vulnerably on your grief journey, *with* your spouse.

You may be asking yourself, "What would it look like to allow myself to be truly seen by my husband and to expose all of my heart to him?" After my children died, being honest with Ryan seemed a little scary. I desperately wanted to turn back time to 2002 and see Ryan again through the eyes of that young bride, walking anxiously down the aisle to say "I do." A smile had adorned my face from ear to ear. Ryan was everything I had dreamed of! How then did I find myself in this place of desolation, sometimes seeing him as the enemy? How did we get there? It can all be chalked up to what grief did to me, or what I allowed grief to do. Slowly, as though a silent leprosy was killing me from the inside out.

In 2017, Ryan and I had a deep conversion experience after I attended a Cursillo weekend—a three-day retreat to deepen my Catholic faith and grow spiritually. Child loss had distorted my identity, and I no longer knew who I was. I did not love myself. In fact, I hated who I had become. There were times when I was so desperate for the pain of grief to go away that I felt as if I was just waiting for my time to die. I didn't want to hurt myself, but I felt really tired and ready to give up. I had white-knuckled my grief for so long, thinking that I had to be sad or I would be doing my children's memory a disservice. After almost a decade, I was desperate to find myself again, and I agreed to attend a Cursillo weekend.

Within a year, we went from being lukewarm Catholics to the crazy Catholics the secular world talks about. We were completely ravished by Jesus's love and healed through the sacraments of the Catholic Church. Through our Cursillo weekends, I realized that we were trying to carry the cross of child loss in mortal sin. I did not have the ability to carry such a heavy cross, I needed God's grace, but I had blocked the flow of that grace when I was living in darkness.

During that weekend retreat, I found a love for Confession and adoration. This set my heart free from the bondage of my sin. My circumstances did not change, I was still a mother of loss, but God transformed my perception and the way I treated my husband and family. It's not good enough to just know who Jesus is; if Jesus does not live inside of you, the light will never prevail over the darkness that resides within. I allowed God's grace and the sacraments to heal and restore me. I took out the wooden beam from my eye so that I could help my family get to heaven (Mt 7:3).

I long to see my children again and strive for holiness every day. I learned to let go of my expectations of Ryan and began to love him again for who he is, not for what he did for me. When I prioritized my relationship with God and allowed him to restore my heart back to grace, I fell in love with Ryan all over again. Love began to be restored every day that I lived out my vocations as daughter, wife, and then mother.

Suffering wasn't over for us. Five years after our conversion, we had another loss. Eva Catherine died in utero at only six weeks. Instantly the pain resurfaced and rushed through our world anew like a tsunami. The night I began to bleed, Ryan followed me into our room, both of us paralyzed by the weight of this new cross. I crawled into our bed and curled into the fetal position while he held my hand. He let me speak my heart out loud through the tears and wailing sobs. I was angry again, but instead of leaving, he got under the covers with me, held me, and we cried this time together. I was no longer alone in the bottomless pit when suffering entered our life. I don't know how long we remained there crying together, but I know that was exactly what we both needed. My heart was broken into a million pieces once again. This time, we clung to each other and to God.

Not long after we lost Eva, we received a text from Sr. Marie Thérèse, a friend of ours, that she was in prayer with our family. She wrote, "God must love you and trust you a lot to let your heart get pierced like his mother's." As I read her text, tears burst from my eyes. I love the Blessed Mother so much, but in those moments, I didn't feel so blessed or loved by the Lord. Death brings you to the brink where truth and reality meet. Once again, the pain of child loss attempted to overcome me.

Our story is filled with suffering, but it is also filled with great joy. Sometimes I believe that I will soar through my pain and grief, carrying our cross. And other times the cross feels like it is dragging us. Sometimes I lament to the Lord in utter disbelief, and sometimes I am freely able to offer all of myself to him—even the devastating pain. As I enter into suffering time and time again, I realize that I no longer feel so alone when my world begins to spin out of control. I know the Lord is close to me and that he slowly stops my teacup from spinning. Even when I feel as if the earth will swallow me whole in an abyss of pain, because I am in sanctifying grace, I no longer feel the isolation and desolation of my grief. Grief does not wreck me like it once did. I can grieve with hope now. I also know that my husband is with me in my grief and together we will figure it out. If nothing else, we will pray together, and when I'm on the floor in tears again, he will pray over me. And on most days, that is enough.

No matter what the future brings, I know where to go. I return to my safe place with the Lord. I close my eyes and I see myself once again at the foot of the Cross. I'm looking up at Our Lord. He is broken. He is bleeding. And sometimes, so am I. I am not alone. Jesus is always with me. As Catholics, we preach Christ crucified; we are Easter people. As a reminder to all, there is no Easter Sunday without Good Friday. Even on Holy Saturday, the earth was dark for a time before glory came, but Jesus made something good out of the darkness, and he will for you too.

No matter where you are in your journey of child loss, it is most important to allow God to love you, but let your husband love you too—the way that he knows how. United in grief, you can rediscover and treasure the gift of your marriage and the gift of love God is restoring between you in and through the death of your beloved child. We know that God did not will our children to die, but he will sanctify us through their death. What we thought was meant for evil, he will make beautiful.

One day soon, I pray, we will be with God in the beatific vision restored completely. Until then, I offer up my suffering for each of you.

19

Advice for a Grieving Father's Brother or Friend

Pray: The most efficacious thing you can do for your brother or friend who has lost a child is to remember him, his family, and his child in your prayers. Consider having a Mass offered for the family, especially for their child if he or she died after the age of reason, which is around seven. Offer a monthly Rosary for your brother or friend. Pray for him daily. Storm heaven for his healing, especially asking some of the saints mentioned in this book to intercede for him. Make a holy hour and offer it for his healing.

Rely on the Holy Spirit: The Holy Spirit is your advocate. Ask the Spirit to guide your conversations with your brother or friend. Pray for an increase in the gift of counsel, that you might truly minister to him with God's love. Perhaps the Holy Spirit will also give you a greater gift for empathy whereby you can enter into his pain even though you may have never lost a child.

Speak: Tell your brother or friend that you are sorry for his loss. Speaking to him face-to-face is best. Or write a card if you don't live nearby. Tell him you are suffering with him and that he is not alone.

Remain in Continual Communication: Stay in touch with your brother or friend. Continue to reach out months and even years after the death of his child. Send him a random text and ask how he is doing. Ask if there is anything you can do for his family. Maybe he could use help with a house project. A true friend doesn't just accompany you to the Cross and then leave. He stays with you in your highs and lows.

Remember: Mark on your calendar the date of the child's death or even the due date if the child died in the womb. Send an email, text, or card on the anniversary. Don't be afraid to speak about your friend's or brother's child. Let him change the subject if he would rather not talk about it.

Encourage Fellowship: Your brother or friend may not want to hang out in large groups, but consider inviting him to play tennis or golf, or to share a beer at your house for some one-on-one time.

Use Prudence: If your wife becomes pregnant, especially if your friend or brother has lost a child in the womb recently, use discretion about sharing that information right away. If you have a son or daughter who is around the same age as his child was, consider that it may be hard for him to hear you talk about your child. It may help to wait for him to somehow signal how comfortable he is or isn't. He may ask at some point how your child is doing, which can be a good indication that he's okay hearing some things. Attend to what your friend or brother says, but also his nonverbals. It's okay to ask him if he would prefer not to discuss something because it might trigger his grief.

Be Patient: Be patient with your brother or friend. Child loss has changed him forever. He is no longer the same person. His heart has been deeply pierced as was Our Lady's. As a result, he may be distant from you because he doesn't want to be around anyone, especially those people who do not understand his pain. Don't take it personally. Give him space, but never give up on him because you are hurt or saddened by his lack of interest. Put yourself in his shoes and help him carry his cross. And don't be afraid to mourn with him. Let him know his tears and grief are welcome, just as he is, no matter how he's doing on any given day. Let him know you are hurting because he is hurting and that you also mourn his child.

20

Advice for a Grieving Father's Pastor

Be a Priestly Presence: To be present to a grieving parent is one of the most difficult works of mercy a priest will undertake in his priestly ministry. To be present means more than celebrating the Funeral Mass—though this is the greatest work a priest can do. It also means being a perpetual visible presence. A priest must offer his listening ear, his steady encouragement, and most of all, be a visible sign of God's mercy and love. While many couples will benefit from the direct ministry of their pastor as a couple, many loss dads will also benefit from individual time spent with their priest.

Remember: Our Lord instituted the Holy Eucharist so that his Church would forever remain united in him through the Holy Sacrifice. The Eucharist makes Christ present and forms us to be his Body in our world. How tragic, then, when people near us, especially our priests, forget about us or neglect to be Christ's Body for us, especially in our greatest sorrow and pain. Child loss is the most bitter chalice of any marriage and likely the greatest test of any person's faith. The notion of a loving and merciful God is quickly challenged. A priest must do everything he can with God's grace not to forget the grieving father and his spouse, lest they leave the sheepfold. Perhaps the priest could mark on his church calendar the date of the child's death and offer to

165

celebrate a Mass for the family and their child. He could remember the anniversary with an email or simple text to the grieving father. If the father has no living children, perhaps the priest could include a special blessing on Father's Day for all fathers of living and deceased children.

Speak: As the psalm says, "My soul thirsts for God" (42:3); so too do we long for life-giving words from our pastors. We appreciate simple statements like "I'm sorry for the loss of your child." Saying the name of the child in expressions of condolence opens the door for conversation or spiritual counsel, or can lead to an invitation to pray together. Sincerely asking, "How are you doing today?" or "Is there something I can do for you?" can heal and keep the door open to further encounters. When a grieving father hears no healing words from his pastor, his grief is untouched. A priest must be like the Good Samaritan in the gospel who goes out of his way to bind up a grieving father's wounds.

Check In: Priests should never assume that time has completely healed the grieving father. Let's face it, only God can heal a broken heart. Healing may take years, and the grief might never go away until heaven. Check in with the grieving father via an email once a month or perhaps a random phone call to see how he is doing, especially in the months after the child's death. Even years later, a priest can do his best to remember his wounded sheep. While an earthly father shows no partiality to his children, he knows that some children require more attention than others—the same is true of spiritual fathers. Those who mourn are particularly vulnerable and worthy of the grace of a pastor's support and guidance.

Counsel: Every priest must allow the Holy Spirit to work through him to offer critical counsel for the grieving father, especially in spiritual direction or in the confessional. If the priest discerns that a grieving father might need professional counseling, he should suggest Catholic or Christian counselors.

Prepare a Homily: Many priests shy away from homilies on child loss. They don't want to conjure up grief or make people uncomfortable. However, preaching on child loss, especially when the *Lectionary* readings mention biblical figures grieving over their children or on the feasts of saints who experienced loss of a child, can be a beautiful way to provide healing from the pulpit.

Encourage: Priests must be a sign of the Resurrection to the grieving father by their joy and in their words. Let the dad know that Our Lord is with him in his suffering and is helping him carry his cross. Let him know that God has a plan even though sometimes it doesn't make sense to us. Telling a grieving father, "You are going to get through this," "God is with you," or "I am here for you," can be very powerful and reassuring, offering him hope and courage in the Lord.

Offer Parish Support: October is child loss awareness month. Especially during this month, consider offering a special holy hour or Mass for parishioners who have lost a child. Additionally, consider instituting a grief support ministry at the parish. The ministry could offer healing retreats or tap into resources available from Red Bird Ministries—the premier Catholic ministry for loss parents.

21

Spiritual Reflections and Prayers

To a Child in Heaven

A. Francis Coomes, SJ

My dear little saint, now alive in heaven, you have gone home to God to be eternally happy and are now in joy in the company of the holy innocents there. It was a thing hard for me to understand when you were taken from us, for parting with you has caused me grief that few can fully understand. Yet in all my grief I am happy, very happy for you, because I know the joy that is yours.

Your joy is now my joy too because I can always feel that I had a part in bringing it to you; and, now that you are in heaven, I realize that you are mine in a truer sense than you could ever be on earth. I cannot lose you now through sin. While parting with you was hard, I would not wish you back because I know that you are happier than I could ever make you were you with me still.

Help me, as you now can with your intercession, that I may be completely faithful to all my duties here below and merit to join you in eternal joys where there will be no more sorrow or parting from those we love. Amen.[1]

Trustful Surrender to Divine Providence
Fr. Jean Baptiste Saint-Jure, SJ, and
St. Claude de la Colombière, SJ

Let us imagine our confusion when we appear before God and understand the reasons why he sent us the crosses we accept so unwillingly. The death of a child will then be seen as its rescue from some great evil had it lived, separation from the woman you love the means of saving you from an unhappy marriage, a severe illness the reason for many years of life afterward, loss of money the means of saving your soul from eternal loss. So what are we worried about? God is looking after us and yet we are full of anxiety. We trust ourselves to a doctor because we suppose he knows his business. He orders an operation which involves cutting away part of our body and we accept it. We are grateful to him and pay him a large fee because we judge he would not act as he does unless the remedy were necessary, and we must rely on his skill. Yet we are unwilling to treat God in the same way! It looks as if we do not trust his wisdom and are afraid he cannot do his job properly. We allow ourselves to be operated on by a man who may easily make a mistake—a mistake which may cost us our life—and protest when God sets to work on us.[2]

How to Converse with God
St. Alphonsus de Liguori

O, my God, all my hopes are in you. I offer you this affliction and conform myself to your Will. But have pity on me, and either deliver me from it or give me strength to suffer it.

Your Cross
St. Francis de Sales

The everlasting God has in his wisdom foreseen from eternity the cross that he now presents to you as a gift from his inmost heart. This cross he now sends you he has considered with his all-knowing eyes, understood with his divine mind, tested with his wise justice, warmed with loving arms, and weighed with his own hands to see that it be not one inch too large and not one ounce too heavy for you. He has blessed it with his Holy Name, anointed it with his consolation, taken one last glance at you and your courage, and then sent it to you from heaven, a special greeting from God to you, alms of the all-merciful love of God.[3]

A Father's Grief

Patrick O'Hearn

My God, my God, why have you forsaken me? These are the words of your beloved Son on the Cross. Father, I feel like your beloved Son on my own Calvary. I feel at times alone, abandoned, broken, and weak because the child whom I love is no more. Is this really happening?

Everything I have been taught about you being loving and merciful is being put to the test. The world has moved on, including most of my family members and friends, but I am still on the Cross. Where are you, Lord? Does anyone understand my pain?

But grace pours forth from your Son's pierced heart. I realize something: I now know how you felt when your Son was dying on the Cross. You grieved just as I am grieving now. And instead of feeling alone on the Cross, your beloved Son is truly embracing me. Yes, Father, he has been with me all along. His outstretched, wounded hands were clinging to me lest I dash my foot against a stone. And your mother is standing behind my cross to catch me when I fall.

Psalm 23

The LORD is my shepherd;
there is nothing I lack.
In green pastures he makes me lie down;
to still waters he leads me;
he restores my soul.
He guides me along right paths
for the sake of his name.
Even though I walk through the valley of the shadow of death,

I will fear no evil, for you are with me;
your rod and your staff comfort me.
You set a table before me
in front of my enemies;
You anoint my head with oil;
my cup overflows.
Indeed, goodness and mercy will pursue me
all the days of my life;
I will dwell in the house of the LORD
for endless days.

Prayer to God the Father

Kelly Breaux

Heavenly Father, we come before you, suffering the loss of our beloved children.

Lord, help us to feel your loving arms wrapped around us. Help us to see your face and to experience your grace. Please quiet our racing hearts and wipe the tears we shed for our children. Lord, we ask that you carry us when we cannot carry ourselves, that you enter into our suffering and unite it with your Son's suffering on the Cross. Lord, we ask that you help us lift our cross high enough to pick it up and run toward you.

Blessed Mother, our beautiful spiritual mother, you know the hearts of your suffering children. Take us in your arms and soothe our suffering hearts. Intercede for us, and petition our Father for healing and for the mercy to feel his presence.

All you angels and saints, please pray for our needs and for our healing. We ask this in Jesus's name. Amen.

Prayer to Our Mother of Sorrows

Patrick O'Hearn

O Mother of Sorrows,
you who once held your son and Our Lord in your blessed arms,

both at his birth and at his death,
look with mercy and compassion on our sufferings
and obtain for us peace in our sorrows.
Please kiss our departed child/children (*name them*) for us
and keep them safe in your mantle until we meet again.
Help us to unite our sufferings with those of Jesus
and obtain for us healing, hope, and perseverance
that we might one day join you forever in heaven
along with all of our family members, friends,
and those in most need of your mercy.
Amen.[4]

The Seven Sorrows of St. Joseph

Fr. Hugolinus Joseph Storff, OFM

1. Doubts about Mary.

2. The lowly poverty of Jesus's birthplace.

3. The circumcision of Jesus, his first blood spilled for us.

4. The prophetic message of Simeon.

5. The flight of the Holy Family into Egypt.

6. The hard trip back from Egypt.

7. The loss of Jesus for three days.

Day 1: St. Joseph, chaste spouse of Mary, great was your sorrow when, in a state of uncertainty, you were inclined to quietly divorce Mary. But great was your joy when the angel revealed to you the mystery of Christ's Incarnation.

By this sorrow and this joy, we ask you to relieve [*name(s)*] of all anxieties and doubts about their future and fill their hearts with confidence in the powerful protection of Mary, the Immaculate Mother of God.

Recite seven Our Fathers and seven Hail Marys.

Day 2: Glorious St. Joseph, chosen foster father of the Word made flesh, great was your sorrow at seeing the Child Jesus born in such poverty. But great was your joy when you beheld the brightness of that holy night in which the angels sang, "Glory to God in the highest and on earth peace to people of goodwill."

By this sorrow and this joy, we implore you to obtain for [*name(s)*] the grace that the Infant Jesus may again be born in their hearts and that, blessed with the sweet peace of God, they may join after their death in the joyful company of the angels.

Recite seven Our Fathers and seven Hail Marys.

Day 3: Glorious St. Joseph, you faithfully obeyed the law of God, and your heart was pierced at the sight of the Precious Blood that was shed by the Infant Savior during his circumcision. But great was your joy when you gave him the name of Jesus that would bring salvation to sinners.

By this sorrow and this joy, obtain for [*name(s)*] the grace to be freed from all sin during life and to die rejoicing with the Holy Name of Jesus in their hearts and on their lips.

Recite seven Our Fathers and seven Hail Marys.

Day 4: Most faithful St. Joseph, great was your sorrow when, at the Presentation of Jesus in the Temple, you heard Simeon's prophecy of the future sufferings of Jesus and Mary. But how great was your joy when Simeon foretold that Jesus would be the light for the revelation to the Gentiles and the glory of his people.

By this sorrow and this joy, we pray that you assist [*name(s)*], that through the light and the power of the Sorrowful Mother, they may see their salvation, and praise and thank God for the grace of a happy death.

Recite seven Our Fathers and seven Hail Marys.

Day 5: Most watchful guardian of the Infant Jesus, great was your sorrow when, obeying the voice of the angel, you fled to Egypt with Mary and the Infant Jesus. But how great was your joy to have God himself with you and to see the idols of the Egyptians fall prostrate before him.

By this sorrow and this joy, I pray that you help [*name(s)*] to banish from their heart all sinful habits so that Jesus and Mary may come and lead their soul(s) to heaven.

Recite seven Our Fathers and seven Hail Marys.

Day 6: Glorious St. Joseph, head and guardian of the Holy Family, great was your sorrow when, upon the return from Egypt, you learned that cruel Archelaus was reigning in Judea. But great was your joy when the angel of God directed you to go to Nazareth, where you lived peacefully with Jesus and Mary until your happy death.

By this sorrow and this joy, I ask that you assist [*name(s)*] that they may overcome all attacks of the evil spirits and die peacefully under the special protection of Jesus and Mary.

Recite seven Our Fathers and seven Hail Marys.

Day 7: Glorious St. Joseph, patron of the dying, great was your sorrow when you lost, through no fault of your own, the Child Jesus for three days. But how great was your joy when you found him in the Temple.

By this sorrow and this joy, we ask you to help [*name(s)*] to not lose their Savior for all eternity, but to find him who is Divine Mercy itself, in the temple of their hearts, especially at the hour of death.

Recite seven Our Fathers and seven Hail Marys.[5]

22

Scripture Passages with Which to Pray

1 Thessalonians 5:16–18—Rejoice always. Pray without ceasing. In all circumstances give thanks, for this is the will of God for you in Christ Jesus.

Romans 12:12—Rejoice in hope, endure in affliction, persevere in prayer.

Revelation 21:4—He will wipe every tear from their eyes, and there shall be no more death or mourning, wailing or pain, [for] the old order has passed away.

Romans 8:18—I consider that the sufferings of this present time are as nothing compared with the glory to be revealed for us.

1 Peter 5:7—Cast all your worries upon him because he cares for you.

Jeremiah 29:11—For I know well the plans I have in mind for you—oracle of the LORD—plans for your welfare and not for woe, so as to give you a future of hope.

2 Corinthians 12:9—He said to me, "My grace is sufficient for you, for power is made perfect in weakness." I will rather boast most gladly of my weaknesses, in order that the power of Christ may dwell with me.

James 1:2–4—Consider it all joy, my brothers, when you encounter various trials, for you know that the testing of your faith produces perseverance. And let perseverance be perfect, so that you may be perfect and complete, lacking in nothing.

Matthew 11:28—Come to me, all you who labor and are burdened, and I will give you rest.

Philippians 4:4–7—Rejoice in the Lord always. I shall say it again: rejoice! Your kindness should be known to all. The Lord is near. Have no anxiety at all, but in everything, by prayer and petition, with thanksgiving, make your requests known to God. Then the peace of God that surpasses all understanding will guard your hearts and minds in Christ Jesus.

John 16:33—I have told you this so that you might have peace in me. In the world you will have trouble, but take courage, I have conquered the world.

Romans 8:28—We know that all things work for good for those who love God, who are called according to his purpose.

Psalm 24:2—My God, in you I trust; do not let me be disgraced.

Part IV
TOOLS FOR THE JOURNEY

Mood-Screening Questionnaires

Sometimes it can be difficult to know whether you need professional help to deal with your grief. The following questionnaires are meant to provide direction for seeking professional counseling or treatment for anxiety, post-traumatic stress disorder, and depression.

Anxiety

The GAD-7 questionnaire is a screening tool for general anxiety disorder.[1] It calculates how many common anxiety symptoms you have and, based on your answers, suggests whether you may have mild, moderate, moderately severe, or severe anxiety. The GAD-7 is not meant to *diagnose* the severity of anxiety—only your doctor can medically diagnose you.

Directions: For each of the seven items, choose one answer from the four columns.

Over the last two weeks, how often have you been bothered by the following problems?	Not at all	Several days	More than half the days	Nearly every day
1. Feeling nervous, anxious, or on edge	0	1	2	3

2. Not able to stop or control worrying	0	1	2	3
3. Worrying too much about different things	0	1	2	3
4. Trouble relaxing	0	1	2	3
5. Being so restless that it's hard to sit still	0	1	2	3
6. Becoming easily annoyed or irritable	0	1	2	3
7. Feeling afraid, as if something awful might happen	0	1	2	3

Add up your results for each column.

Total score (sum column totals)				

Interpretation: If your score is 10 or higher, or if you feel that anxiety is affecting your daily life, call your doctor for further examination. **If you are concerned about your mood or are having thoughts of self-harm, please contact your doctor immediately.**

Post-Traumatic Stress Disorder

The SPRINT questionnaire is a screening tool for post-traumatic stress disorder that asks about symptom severity over the last week.[2]

Directions: For each of the eight items, choose one answer from the five columns.

In the past week . . .	Not at all	A little bit	Moderately	Quite a lot	Very much
1. How much have you been bothered by unwanted memories, nightmares, or reminders of the event?	0	1	2	3	4
2. How much effort have you made to avoid thinking or talking about the event, or doing things that remind you of what happened?	0	1	2	3	4
3. To what extent have you lost enjoyment for things, kept your distance from people, or found it difficult to experience feelings?	0	1	2	3	4
4. How much have you been bothered by poor sleep, poor concentration, jumpiness, irritability, or feeling watchful around you?	0	1	2	3	4
5. How much have you been bothered by pain, body aches, or tiredness?	0	1	2	3	4
6. How much would you get upset when stressful events or setbacks happen to you?	0	1	2	3	4

7. How much have the above symptoms interfered with your ability to work or carry out daily activities?	0	1	2	3	4
8. How much have the above symptoms interfered with your relationships with family or friends?	0	1	2	3	4

Add up your results for each column.

Total score (sum column totals)					

Interpretation: If your score is 17 or higher, or if you feel that these trauma symptoms are affecting your daily life, call your doctor for further evaluation. **If you are concerned about your mood or are having thoughts of self-harm, please contact your doctor immediately.**

Depression

The PHQ-2 is a screening tool that asks about the frequency of depressed mood and inability to feel pleasure over the past two weeks.[3] The PHQ-2 is not meant to diagnose depression severity.

Directions: For each of the two items, choose one answer from the four columns.

Over the last two weeks, how often have you been bothered by the following problems?	Not at all	Several days	More than half the days	Nearly every day
1. Little interest or pleasure in doing things	0	1	2	3

2. Feeling down, depressed, or hopeless	0	1	2	3

Add up your results for each column.

Total score (sum column totals)				

Interpretation: If your score is 3 or higher, or if you feel that depression is affecting your daily life, call your doctor for further evaluation. **If you are concerned about your mood or are having thoughts of self-harm, please contact your doctor immediately.**

Space for Notes or Journaling

This space is for you to use as you need. If you feel prompted, write your thoughts, questions, and prayers. Or consider writing your own story.

The following questions can help you get started:

- How are you hurting?
- What triggers your grief?
- Have you had glimpses of healing?
- What helps you heal?
- Have you opened up to your wife?
- Have you fully expressed your true feelings to God?
- Have you allowed yourself to grieve?
- What do you think God is trying to teach you in your suffering?
- Who can you help that is hurting? How does the hope of eternal life and seeing your child again keep you going?
- Who are some saints whom you can invoke, particularly those found in this book, who can help you in your grief?
- Were there any particular stories in this book that touched you, and how so?

_____

_____

_____

_____

_____

_____

_____

_____

_____

_____

_____

_____

_____

_____

_____

_____

_____

_____

_____

_____

_____

_____

_____

_____

_____

_____

Additional Resources

Consoling Thoughts on God and Providence, by St. Francis de Sales, will help you love God's divine plan in your life.

Hiding in the Upper Room, by Kelly Breaux, relates a mother and wife's experience of grief in child loss.

Nursery of Heaven, by Cassie Everts and Patrick O'Hearn, is a book for Catholic couples who have experienced miscarriage, stillbirth, or infant loss.

Presence of God, The, by Anselm Moynihan, OP, will help you understand and experience the real and indwelling presence of God in you.

Red Bird Ministries is a nonprofit Catholic grief support ministry serving individuals and couples who have experienced child loss from pregnancy through adulthood (http://redbird.love).

Searching for and Maintaining Peace, by Fr. Jacques Philippe, reveals how to abandon yourself to God's loving care in order to obtain peace.

Trustful Surrender to Divine Providence, by Fr. Jean Baptiste Saint-Jure, SJ, and St. Claude de la Colombière, SJ, is a small but powerful book that reveals the only way to have true peace in life.

Uniformity with God's Will, by St. Alphonsus de Liguori, explains how to perfectly love God by completely uniting your will with his.

When a Loved One Dies by Suicide: Comfort, Hope, and Healing for Grieving Catholics and *Responding to Suicide: A Pastoral Handbook for Catholic Leaders* by the Association of Catholic Mental Health Ministers, compilers and editors Ed Shoener and John P. Dolan both take a holistic approach to understanding and responding to suicide loss in ways carefully aligned with mental health experts and the teaching of the Catholic Church.

www.catholictherapists.com is an online resource that will help you find a Catholic therapist.

Notes

1. Male Grief Examined

1. K. L. Obst, C. Due, M. Oxlad, and P. Middleton, "Men's Grief following Pregnancy Loss and Neonatal Loss: A Systematic Review and Emerging Theoretical Model," *BMC Pregnancy and Childbirth* 20, no. 11 (2020), doi:10.1186/s12884-019-2677-9.

2. Obst et al., "Men's Grief following Pregnancy Loss"; J. E. Lawn et al., "Stillbirths: Where? When? Why? How to Make the Data Count?" *Lancet* 377 (2011): 1448–63, doi:10.1016/S0140-6736(10)62187-3.

3. WHO, "Infant Mortality," https://www.who.int/data/gho/data/themes/topics/indicator-groups/indicator-group-details/GHO/infant-mortality.

4. K. L. Obst and C. Due, "Australian Men's Experiences of Support following Pregnancy Loss: A Qualitative Study," *Midwifery* 70 (2019): 1–6, doi:10.1016/j.midw.2018.11.013; N. Dias, S. Docherty, and D. Brandon, "Parental Bereavement: Looking beyond Grief," *Death Studies* 41 (2017): 318–27, doi:10.1080/07481187.2017.1279239.

5. M. Beutel, H. Willner, R. Deckardt, M. Von Rad, and H. Weiner, "Similarities and Differences in Couples' Grief Reactions following a Miscarriage: Results from a Longitudinal Study," *Journal of Psychosomatic Research* 40 (1996): 245–53, doi:10.1016/0022-3999(95)00520-x.

6. Beutel et al., "Similarities and Differences."

7. K. Jones, M. Robb, S. Murphy, and A. Davies, "New Understandings of Fathers' Experiences of Grief and Loss following Stillbirth and Neonatal Death: A Scoping Review," *Midwifery* 79 (2019), doi:10.1016/j.midw.2019.102531.

8. Obst et al., "Men's Grief following Pregnancy Loss"; L. D. M. Lizcano Pabon, M. E. Moreno Fergusson, and A. M. Palacios, "Experience of Perinatal Death from the Father's Perspective," *Nursing Research* 68 (2019): E1–E9, doi:10.1097/NNR.0000000000000369.

9. Jones et al., "New Understandings."

10. K. Conway and G. Russell, "Couples' Grief and Experience of Support in the Aftermath of Miscarriage," *British Journal of Medical Psychology* 73, pt. 4 (2000):

531–45, doi:10.1348/000711200160714; M. P. Johnson and J. E. Puddifoot, "The Grief Response in the Partners of Women Who Miscarry," *British Journal of Medical Psychology* 69, pt. 4 (1996): 313–27, doi:10.1111/j.2044-8341.1996.tb01875.x.

11. Obst et al., "Men's Grief following Pregnancy Loss."

12. Obst et al., "Men's Grief following Pregnancy Loss"; E. J. Miller, M. J. Temple-Smith, and J. E. Bilardi, "'There Was Just No-One There to Acknowledge That It Happened to Me as Well': A Qualitative Study of Male Partner's Experience of Miscarriage," *PLOS One* 14 (2019): e0217395, doi:10.1371/journal.pone.0217395.

13. H. Volgsten, C. Jansson, A. S. Svanberg, E. Darj, and A. Stavreus-Evers, "Longitudinal Study of Emotional Experiences, Grief and Depressive Symptoms in Women and Men after Miscarriage," *Midwifery* 64 (2018): 23–28, doi:10.1016/j.midw.2018.05.003.

14. J. O'Leary and C. Thorwick, "Fathers' Perspectives during Pregnancy, Postperinatal Loss," *Journal of Obstetric, Gynecologic & Neonatal Nursing* 35 (2006): 78–86, doi:10.1111/j.1552-6909.2006.00017.x.

15. Volgsten et al., "Longitudinal Study."

16. Obst and Due, "Australian Men's Experiences of Support"; Dias, Docherty, and Brandon, "Parental Bereavement."

17. Volgsten et al., "Longitudinal Study"; C. S. Huffman, T. A. Schwartz, and K. M. Swanson, "Couples and Miscarriage: The Influence of Gender and Reproductive Factors on the Impact of Miscarriage," *Women's Health Issues* 25 (2015): 570–78, doi:10.1016/j.whi.2015.04.005; Y. F. Tseng, H. R. Cheng, Y. P. Chen, S. F. Yang, and P. T. Cheng, "Grief Reactions of Couples to Perinatal Loss: A One-Year Prospective Follow-Up," *Journal of Clinical Nursing* 26 (2017): 5133–42, doi:10.1111/jocn.14059.

18. Obst et al., "Men's Grief following Pregnancy Loss."

19. Volgsten et al., "Longitudinal Study"; D. Armstrong, "Exploring Fathers' Experiences of Pregnancy after a Prior Perinatal Loss," *MCN: The American Journal of Maternal/Child Nursing* 26 (2001): 147–53, doi:10.1097/00005721-200105000-00012.

20. C. Burden et al., "From Grief, Guilt, Pain and Stigma to Hope and Pride: A Systematic Review and Meta-analysis of Mixed-Method Research of the Psychosocial Impact of Stillbirth," *BMC Pregnancy and Childbirth* 16 (2016): 9, doi:10.1186/s12884-016-0800-8.

21. Burden et al., "From Grief, Guilt, Pain and Stigma to Hope and Pride."

22. Miller et al., "There Was Just No-One There."

23. Johnson and Puddifoot, "The Grief Response."

24. P. Martinez-Serrano, A. Pedraz-Marcos, M. Solis-Munoz, and A. M. Palmar-Santos, "The Experience of Mothers and Fathers in Cases of Stillbirth in Spain: A Qualitative Study," *Midwifery* 77 (2019): 37–44, doi:10.1016/j.midw.2019.06.013.

25. D. Nuzum, S. Meaney, and K. O'Donoghue, "The Impact of Stillbirth on Bereaved Parents: A Qualitative Study," *PLOS One* 13 (2018): e0191635, doi:10.1371/journal.pone.0191635.

26. Burden et al., "From Grief, Guilt, Pain and Stigma to Hope and Pride."

27. Burden et al., "From Grief, Guilt, Pain and Stigma to Hope and Pride."

28. Beutel et al., "Similarities and Differences."

29. Burden et al., "From Grief, Guilt, Pain and Stigma to Hope and Pride"; P. Turton et al., "Psychological Impact of Stillbirth on Fathers in the Subsequent Pregnancy and Puerperium," *British Journal of Psychiatry* 188 (2006): 165–72, doi:10.1192/bjp.188.2.165.

30. Dias, Docherty, and Brandon, "Parental Bereavement"; Jones et al., "New Understandings"; Turton et al., "Psychological Impact of Stillbirth."

31. Dias, Docherty, and Brandon, "Parental Bereavement."

32. Dias, Docherty, and Brandon, "Parental Bereavement."

33. Obst et al., "Men's Grief following Pregnancy Loss"; Lizcano Pabon et al., "Experience of Perinatal Death."

34. Volgsten et al., "Longitudinal Study."

35. Miller et al., "There Was Just No-One There"; Burden et al., "From Grief, Guilt, Pain and Stigma to Hope and Pride."

36. Miller et al., "There Was Just No-One There."

37. Miller et al., "There Was Just No-One There."

38. Obst et al., "Men's Grief following Pregnancy Loss."

39. Obst et al., "Men's Grief following Pregnancy Loss"; Burden et al., "From Grief, Guilt, Pain and Stigma to Hope and Pride."

40. Dias, Docherty, and Brandon, "Parental Bereavement."

41. Obst et al., "Men's Grief following Pregnancy Loss."

42. Burden et al., "From Grief, Guilt, Pain and Stigma to Hope and Pride."

43. Burden et al., "From Grief, Guilt, Pain and Stigma to Hope and Pride."

44. Tseng et al., "Grief Reactions."

45. Turton et al., "Psychological Impact of Stillbirth."

46. Miller et al., "There Was Just No-One There"; Burden et al., "From Grief, Guilt, Pain and Stigma to Hope and Pride."

47. Dias, Docherty, and Brandon, "Parental Bereavement."

48. Dias, Docherty, and Brandon, "Parental Bereavement."

49. Obst et al., "Men's Grief following Pregnancy Loss"; Martinez-Serrano et al., "The Experience of Mothers and Fathers in Cases of Stillbirth."

50. Martinez-Serrano et al., "The Experience of Mothers and Fathers in Cases of Stillbirth."

51. Miller et al., "There Was Just No-One There."

52. Obst et al., "Men's Grief following Pregnancy Loss."

53. Obst et al., "Men's Grief following Pregnancy Loss."

54. Martinez-Serrano et al., "The Experience of Mothers and Fathers in Cases of Stillbirth."

55. Obst et al., "Men's Grief following Pregnancy Loss."

56. Miller et al., "There Was Just No-One There."

57. Miller et al., "There Was Just No-One There."

2. Child Loss in the Bible

1. Henri-Paul Bergeron, CSC, *Brother André: The Wonder Man of Mount Royal*, trans. Real Boudreau (Montreal: Fides, 1969), 104–5.

3. Loss Dads among the Saints

1. Mary of Agreda, *The Mystical City of God* (Charlotte, NC: TAN Books, 1978), 295–96.

2. Augustine of Hippo, *The Confessions of St. Augustine* (Totowa, NJ: Catholic Book Publishing Corp., 1997), 256.

3. Ibid.

4. "Blessed Henry of Treviso," CatholicSaints.Info, catholicsaints.info/blessed-henry-of-treviso/.

5. Zélie and Louis Martin, *A Call to a Deeper Love: The Family Correspondence of the Parents of St. Thérèse of the Child Jesus, 1863–1885*, ed. Frances Renda (New York: Society of St. Paul, 2011), 91.

6. Thérèse of Lisieux, *Story of a Soul* (Washington, DC: ICS Publications, 1996), 87.

7. "Saint Teresa of Avila Quotes," Carmel, Garden of God, carmelourladysdovecote.wordpress.com/2012/08/26/st-teresa-of-avila-quotes/.

8. Slawomir Oder and Saverio Gaeta, *Why He Is a Saint*, trans. Antony Shugaar (New York: Rizzoli, 2010), 12.

9. André Frossard, *"Be Not Afraid!": John Paul Speaks Out on His Life, His Beliefs, and His Inspiring Vision for Humanity*, trans. J. R. Foster (New York: St. Martin's Press, 1984), 14.

4. Miscarriage: Surrender Is the Only Path to His Heart

1. International Theological Commission, "The Hope of Salvation for Infants Who Die without Being Baptised," https://www.vatican.va/roman_curia/congregations/cfaith/cti_documents/rc_con_cfaith_doc_20070419_un-baptised-infants_en.html.

2. "Quotes on Suffering," Catholic Miscarriage Support, https://www.catholicmiscarriagesupport.com/emotional/quotes-on-suffering/.

3. Alphonsus de Liguori, *The Passion and the Death of Jesus Christ* (New York: Benzinger Brothers, 1887), 38.

5. Miscarriage: Pray without Ceasing

1. Alphonsus de Liguori, *Meditations and Readings for Every Day of the Year* (Dublin: Talbot Press, 1928), vol. 3, pt. 1, 186.

9. Losing a Young Child: Radical Acceptance

1. These fertility shots were taken before we reverted back to the faith. They are not permitted by the Catholic Church.

13. Losing an Adult Child: No Greater Love

1. Dan Culloton, "Rock Island Prays for Missing Airman," *Chicago Tribune*, February 21, 1991, www.chicagotribune.com/news/ct-xpm-1991-02-21-9101160903-story.html.

2. The Silver Star is the US armed forces's third-highest military decoration for valor in combat.

3. While on a top mission to strike one of Saddam Hussein's strategic oil fields, Robert Sweet's plane was shot down. Instead of retreating, Captain Stephen hovered for three minutes and forty-five seconds to try to divert bullets from Robert's jet, so that Robert might not get shot while parachuting or become a POW. Brian W. Everstine tells this remarkable story in "Above and Beyond: The Fight to Upgrade One Airman's Silver Star," *Air & Space Forces Magazine*, March 26, 2021, https://www.airforcemag.com/article/above-and-beyond/. Rob became a POW for nineteen days but was eventually released. Captain Stephen was thought to have been unconscious as he did not eject before his aircraft hit Iraqi soil.

17. Advice for a Grieving Father

1. Gabrielle Bossis, *He and I*, trans. Evelyn M. Brown (Boston: Pauline Books, 2013), 113.

21. Spiritual Reflections and Prayers

1. A. Francis Coomes, SJ, *Fathers' Manual* (Cumberland, RI: William J. Hirten Co., 1994), 65.

2. Jean Baptiste Saint-Jure, SJ, and St. Claude de la Colombière, SJ, *Trustful Surrender to Divine Providence* (Charlotte, NC: TAN Books, 2012), 89–90.

3. St. Frances de Sales, "Your Cross," Catholic Online, https://www.catholic.org/prayers/prayer.php?p=52.

4. Cassie Everts and Patrick O'Hearn, *Nursery of Heaven: Miscarriage, Stillbirth, and Infant Loss in the Lives of the Saints and Today's Parents* (Raleigh, NC: Contemplative Heart Press, 2019), 175.

5. "St. Joseph's Seven Sorrows and Seven Joys," The Divine Mercy, https://www.thedivinemercy.org/articles/st-josephs-seven-sorrows-and-seven-joys.

Mood-Screening Questionnaires

1. Robert L. Spitzer, MD, Kurt Kroenke, MD, Janet B. W. Williams, DSW, and Bernd Löwe, MD, PhD, "A Brief Measure for Assessing Generalized Anxiety Disorder: The GAD-7," *Archives of Internal Medicine* 166, no. 10 (2006): 1092–97, doi:10.1001/archinte.166.10.1092.

2. K. M. Connor and J. R. Davidson, "SPRINT: A Brief Global Assessment of Post-Traumatic Stress Disorder," *International Clinical Psychopharmacology* 16, no. 5 (2001): 279–84, doi: 10.1097/00004850-200109000-00005. PMID: 11552771.

3. K. Kroenke, R. L. Spitzer, and J. B. Williams, "The Patient Health Questionnaire-2: Validity of a Two-Item Depression Screener," *Medical Care* 41 (2003): 1284–92.

Bibliography

Augustine of Hippo. *The Confessions of St. Augustine*. Totowa, NJ: Catholic Book Publishing, 1997.

Bergeron, Henri-Paul, CSC. *Brother André: The Wonder Man of Mount Royal*. Translated by Real Boudreau. Montreal: Fides, 1969.

Bossis, Gabrielle. *He and I*. Translated by Evelyn M. Brown. Boston: Pauline Books, 2013.

Coomes, A. Francis, SJ. *Fathers' Manual*. Cumberland, RI: William J. Hirten, 1994.

de Liguori, Alphonsus. *Meditations and Readings for Every Day of the Year*. Dublin: Talbot Press, 1928.

_____. *The Passion and the Death of Jesus Christ*. New York: Benzinger Brothers, 1887.

Everts, Cassie, and Patrick O'Hearn. *Nursery of Heaven: Miscarriage, Stillbirth, and Infant Loss in the Lives of the Saints and Today's Parents*. Raleigh, NC: Contemplative Heart Press, 2019.

Frossard, André. *"Be Not Afraid!": John Paul Speaks Out on His Life, His Beliefs, and His Inspiring Vision for Humanity*. Translated by J. R. Foster. New York: St. Martin's Press, 1984.

Martin, Zélie and Louis. *A Call to a Deeper Love: The Family Correspondence of the Parents of St. Thérèse of the Child Jesus, 1863–1885*. Edited by Frances Renda. New York: Society of St. Paul, 2011.

Mary of Agreda, *The Mystical City of God*. Charlotte, NC: TAN Books, 1978.

Oder, Slawomir, and Saverio Gaeta. *Why He Is a Saint*. Translated by Antony Shugaar. New York: Rizzoli, 2010.

Saint-Jure Jean Baptiste, SJ, and St. Claude de la Colombière, SJ. *Trustful Surrender to Divine Providence*. Charlotte, NC: TAN Books, 2012.

Thérèse of Lisieux, *Story of a Soul*. Washington, DC: ICS Publications, 1996.

Patrick O'Hearn is a Catholic author of several books, including *Nursery of Heaven: Miscarriage, Stillbirth, and Infant Loss in the Lives of the Saints and Today's Parents.*

He earned a bachelor's degree from St. Ambrose University and a master's degree from Franciscan University of Steubenville. O'Hearn is a member of the Knights of Columbus. He founded Contemplative Heart Press and serves as a freelance editor with TAN Books.

His work has been featured in the *National Catholic Register* and *Aleteia.* O'Hearn has appeared on EWTN's *Women of Grace* and *At Home with Jim and Joy*, EWTN radio, Relevant Radio, and Iowa Catholic Radio.

He and his wife, Amanda, lost two of their four children to miscarriage.

www.contemplativeheartpress.com

Bryan Feger is a scientist and medical writer. He earned a bachelor's degree from Augustana College and a doctorate in physiology from the University of North Carolina at Greensboro.

He is a member of the Knights of Columbus and serves as a high school catechist and as part of Yokefellows Prison Ministry.

After experiencing the loss of three children from miscarriage, he feels called to let other dads know they are not alone, grieving is necessary, and healing is possible.

Kelly and **Ryan Breaux** cofounded Red Bird Ministries following the loss of four of their children—two boys and two girls. The organization helps parents who have lost a child to find healing. Red Bird partners with dioceses and parishes to provide the tools and resources to support families who have experienced the loss of a child from pregnancy through adulthood.

Ryan and Kelly coauthored *Restoring Love*. Ryan also contributed to several books published by Red Bird Ministries for group and couple's programs offered by the organization. Ryan and Kelly provide mental health content for the Hallow app. They have been guests on a number of Catholic radio and TV shows, including *At Home with Jim and Joy* on EWTN, Rome Reports, the Catholic Faith Network, *Seize the Day with Gus Lloyd*, and *Kresta in the Afternoon*. Their work has been featured in the *National Catholic Register*, *Radiant* magazine, FemCatholic, Aleteia, and in numerous diocesan publications.

Ryan works as a key account manager for Coca-Cola Bottling Company United and is in his second term as an alderman. He is a member of the Knights of Columbus.

www.redbird.love
Facebook: @redbirdministrylove
Instagram: @redbirdministriesinc
Pinterest: @redbird.love
YouTube: @redbirdministries

Ave Maria Press

Founded in 1865, Ave Maria Press,
a ministry of the Congregation of
Holy Cross, is a Catholic publishing
company that serves the spiritual and
formative needs of the Church and its
schools, institutions, and ministers;
Christian individuals and families; and
others seeking spiritual nourishment.

———— ⊷◉⊶ ————

For a complete listing of titles from

Ave Maria Press

Sorin Books

Forest of Peace

Christian Classics

visit www.avemariapress.com

AVE MARIA PRESS
Notre Dame, IN
A Ministry of the United States Province of Holy Cross